HOLGER WINDELOV'S
TROPICA COLOR CATALOGUE

AQUARIUM PLANTS

Accompanying text by
Jiri Stodola

Cryptocoryne pontederiifolia, from Sumatra.

Cryptocoryne ferrugin

Cryptocoryne longicauda

Cryptocoryne schulzei, from Malaysia.

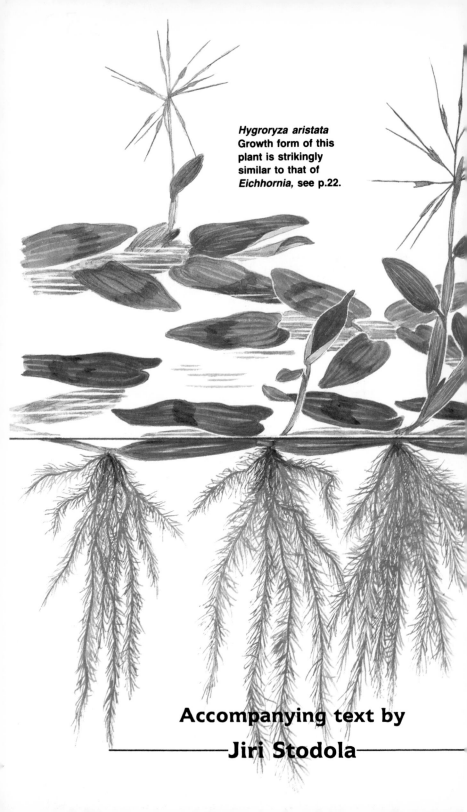

Hygroryza aristata
Growth form of this plant is strikingly similar to that of *Eichhornia*, see p.22.

Accompanying text by
Jiri Stodola

HOLGER WINDELOV'S
TROPICA COLOR CATALOGUE

AQUARIUM
PLANTS

Contents/Index

Page numbers shown in **boldface** type refer to illustrations. Entries shown in **BOLDFACE CAPITALS** refer to major sections of the text.

© **1987 by T.F.H. Publications, Inc.**

Distributed in the UNITED STATES by T.F.H. Publications, Inc., 211 West Sylvani Avenue, Neptune City, NJ 07753; in CANADA to the Pet Trade by H & L Pet Sup plies Inc., 27 Kingston Crescent, Kitchener, Ontario N2B 2T6; Rolf C. Hagen Ltd 3225 Sartelon Street, Montreal 382 Quebec; in CANADA to the Book Trade b Macmillan of Canada (A Division of Canada Publishing Corporation), 164 Com mander Boulevard, Agincourt, Ontario M1S 3C7; in ENGLAND by T.F.H. Public tions Limited, 4 Kier Park, Ascot, Berkshire SL5 7DS; in AUSTRALIA AND TH SOUTH PACIFIC by T.F.H. (Australia) Pty. Ltd., Box 149, Brookvale 2100 N.S.W Australia; in NEW ZEALAND by Ross Haines & Son, Ltd., 18 Monmouth Stree Grey Lynn, Auckland 2 New Zealand; in SINGAPORE AND MALAYSIA by MP Distributors (S) Pte., Ltd., 601 Sims Drive, #03/07/21, Singapore 1438; in th PHILIPPINES by Bio-Research, 5 Lippay Street, San Lorenzo Village, Makati Riza in SOUTH AFRICA by Multipet Pty. Ltd., 30 Turners Avenue, Durban 4001. Pu lished by T.F.H. Publications Inc. Manufactured in the United States of Americ by T.F.H. Publications, Inc.

Introduction

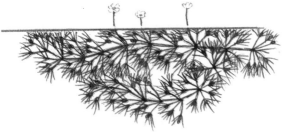

Aldrovanda vesiculosa, a rare floating water plant that is carnivorous like *Utricularia*, see p.24.

Aquarium plants are water or bog plants, either with flowers produced underwater, floating on the surface, or partly growing above the surface. They are cultivated in a reduced space (an aquarium) or in an artificial locality in the open (pools, lakes, garden pools and tanks). The tanks are usually occupied by fish which are also kept there.

Some species have adapted very well to these conditions for a long time (*Elodea, Vallisneria*), but new and interesting species are always turning up which are highly suitable for the aquarium.

The Importance of Aquarium Plants

The function of plants in the aquarium has long been exaggerated, but it is a fact that they help in promoting biologic circulation in the water and help in providing a source of oxygen and organic matter. They also help consume carbon dioxide and other fish wastes during photosynthesis.

In a purely decorative sense, they form a vivid background to accentuate the underwater picture presented by the aquarium. They often serve as a repository for spawned fish eggs and a hiding place for small fry, as well as providing a shelter for living infusoria, an important food in a fish's first stages of growth.

Aquarium plants are also very interesting objects for botanical study. They are very adaptable to changing and react by conforming their shapes to adjust to their new living conditions. A knowledge of the biology of aquarium plants is a very useful thing for aquarists when setting up a tank, and this phase of aquarium science has been given a great deal more attention now than formerly. It is no longer enough merely to keep plants in the aquarium. The thorough aquarist wants to identify them correctly, know where they are native and how they propagate in the aquarium and how much light and temperature are required. With the newer plant species this knowledge may very well be new to science and the hobby as well, because at times only the sparsest information is available from collectors.

Ricciocarpus natans, a decorative floating species of thallose livewort.

8

The Life of Aquarium Plants

A plant in the aquarium is not only a static object for observation but a dynamic living organism. To become well acquainted with aquarium plants, we should know their life cycle, beginning with germination through the development of leaves and blossoms to the sexual propagation, pollination and the development of seeds. We would do well to study the influence of the changing vegetative conditions, such as lowering the water level, giving rise to terrestrial phases. These phases are considerably different from the aquatic forms usually found in the aquarium. Most of the aquatic life processes, however, can easily be duplicated by providing the proper conditions (light, temperature, volume of water, etc.).

Green aquarium plants are assimilators. Under the influence of light on the chlorophyll they are capable of producing organic substances (sugars, starches and albumen). At the same time they assimilate carbon dioxide in the water and in turn produce oxygen. The opposite of this process, dissimilation, takes place when the light is no longer there. This exchange of gases usually takes place in the water, but if the plant has a floating leaf it takes place in the air. A floating plant, therefore, has little effect in enriching the water with oxygen.

Water plants receive their nutriments (inorganic matter), water and a dissolved carbon dioxide on their entire structural surface. They resist absorption of water with their outer skin; they develop their own air space in a spongy tissue inside the body, which has a gaseous content different from the atmospheric air.

Aquatic plants make use of dissolved carbonic acid and bicarbonates. They also require fundamental elements like oxygen, carbon, nitrogen, phosphorus, sulphur, sodium, potassium, calcium, magnesium and iron, as well as tiny amounts of copper and zinc. The plant receives all these elements electively, choosing only a certain amount of the ones needed. After some time there may occur a deficiency of nitrogen and phosphorus or even some other important elements in the aquarium. Water plants also have the ability to concentrate certain elements in their bodies (as for instance, the water chestnut, which stores manganese).

***Phyllanthus fluitans*, a free-floating plant.**

Water plants also have a special affinity for the characteristics of the water from which they come. Some species prosper in eutrophic waters (hard, alkaline) with a high percentage of nutriments and calcium (*Nuphar luteum, Nitella flexilis, Potamogeton crispus, Ceratophyllum demersum*), while other types flourish in dystrophic water (soft, acid) without calcium but with a great percentage of humic acid (*Isoetes lacustris, Cryptocoryne griffithii, Sphagnum cuspidatum, Utricularia vulgaris*). Then there is a large group of water plants which live in oligotrophic waters which have a neutral pH value. The choice of a suitable bottom is more important here.

Ecological Conditions

Limnobium laevigatum, see p.21.

Besides there are fresh, brackish and salt waters where plants react favorably to their surroundings (*Vallisneria neotropicalis, Samolus valerandi*, etc.) The species are more dependent on their bottom in natural waters than they would be in the aquarium and it may be mentioned here that many aquarium plants adapt well to a neutral bottom.

Many types of aquarium plants are known and for classification we can split them into separate groups. Those that we consider alkaline species are kept with a relatively high concentration of hydrogen ions (pH 7.0 to 10.0) in eutrophic water; acid species with a low pH value (5.0 to 7.0) in dystrophic water; and oligotrophic species with a neutral pH value (7.0).

The content of salts of magnesium and calcium in water gives us a feature in water called hardness. A German degree of hardness (DH) is equal to 10 mg. of calcium or 7.2 mg. of magnesium in one liter.

Roughly, 1 DH can be said to be equal to 18 parts per million, which is the usual way of measuring water hardness.

Ecological Conditions

The following main factors affect the life of aquarium plants: *Light, temperature, water depth, the content of nutrients and gases, hydrostatic pressure and water movement.*

Light requirement is important for most aquarium plants. Light which enters the water is diffused, the rays being mostly reflected at the surface. The transparent aquarium sides help compensate for the lack of top light to a great extent.

Temperature is important, especially with tropical species. In the home aquarium, temperature fluctuations are minimized by using a thermostatically controlled heater.

Other influences are usually unimportant. The usual aquarium bottom consists of coarse gravel. Special mixtures are needed with certain species. It is necessary to stress that an experienced aquarist can recognize species with a low, middle or high adaptability to aquarium conditions.

The Inner Structure

The inner structure of an aquarium plant is greatly modified to conform to its environment. These changes may be quite far reaching. The following plant structures are worthy of close study.

The axis The pulp consists of the *aerenchyma* (a spongy mass with large intercellular spaces). There is only one bundle of veins located in the middle of the stem. There is always the endodermis single layer of living cells, usually with thickened radial walls) around this bundle of veins. The vein bundle radiating from the leaves join the main bundle at the nodes (the points at which the

Bolbitis heudelotii, a water fern that originates from Guinea, Africa.

leaves are inserted). This type of bundle appears with *Potamogeton, Elodea, Najas, Ceratophyllum, Myriophyllum* and *Callitriche.*

The root There is no calyptra (root cap) in aquarium plants. Root hairs appear *only* when a plant has been growing in mud. Instead we find *aerenchyma* because there are intercellular canals in the middle tissue. The roots have a greatly reduced vein bundle, especially in the pulpy part. There is only one vein, however, surrounded by the layer of a *phloem* (food-conducting tube) in the center of the roots of *Elodea* and *Vallisneria.*

The leaf The *cuticle* (skin covering) is thin, the *chloroplasts* (cells which contain chlorophyll) occurring only in the epidermis (the outer skin). Water plants only have pores on the upper side; there are no pores on the leaves that remain under water. These plants have a singular leaf structure. A blade of *Elodea,* for example, consists of only two layers of epidermis; its leaves have a sufficiency of chloroplasts. On the other hand, plants of the genus *Potamogeton* have underwater leaves with only one layer of mesophyll (green leaf surface layers).

The Outer Structure
The outer structure of an aquarium plant is also very variable, except for the vital organs which have conformed to water conditions. Shapes are very plastic, especially with heterophylly (leaves of more than one form on the same stem). The genus *Sagittaria,* for instance, grows three types of leaves: aquatic, floating and aerial. There are different ways that organs are reduced. Sometimes no roots

exist (*Utricularia, Ceratophyllum*), or the entire axis is reduced (*Sagittaria, Vallisneria*), sometimes even the leaves (*Wolffia, Lemna*).

We call the *created* morphological types the *biological types* here and they serve to give us the morphological differentiation in our systematic classification. It is simpler for aquarists and they can orient themselves without any detailed botanical knowledge which would otherwise be necessary to get other clues for a determination.

Pilularia globulifera, good in terrariums.

We can recognize three ecological phases which cause changes by the influence of the depth of the water:
1. The aquatic phase—with quite submerged varieties, mostly aquatic species.
2. The littoral phase—with varieties partly emerged above the water surface.
3. The terrestrial phase— terrestrial types, where the water no longer has such great importance.

Microsorium pteropus, see
p.120.

Kinds of Aquatic Plants

The following biological types are artificial keys to groups of aquatic plants. They are presented here only as an identification guide for aquarists.

Biological type 1 Small plants floating on the surface of the water (pleustonic types). They have some parts reduced (roots, leaves) and for nourishment they are dependent on dissolved matter in the water. They are freely floating and do not root, so they change their position with every slight movement of the water.

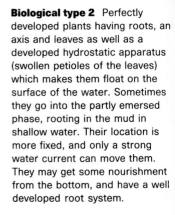

Bacopa caroliniana, see p.92.

Biological type 2 Perfectly developed plants having roots, an axis and leaves as well as a developed hydrostatic apparatus (swollen petioles of the leaves) which makes them float on the surface of the water. Sometimes they go into the partly emersed phase, rooting in the mud in shallow water. Their location is more fixed, and only a strong water current can move them. They may get some nourishment from the bottom, and have a well developed root system.

Biological type 3 Truly submersed plants. They are strictly dependent on the water. They flower in the water as well as being pollinated there, and the fruits ripen there. They perish rather quickly in the partly emersed stage. The leaves are divided into small segments which broaden at the surface, assimilating the diffused light in this way.

Biological type 4 Submersed plants with long leaves which are thread-shaped (*Eleocharis*) or ribbon-shaped (*Vallisneria*) creating a rosette. They root in the bottom and flower on the surface of the water.

Biological type 5 Plants with their leaves submersed and with distinct petiole and the blade. They always flower *above* the water. The genus *Aponogeton* rarely develops terrestrial forms; the genus *Cryptocoryne* turns into a partly emersed to terrestrial form, but requires a damp atmosphere.

Biological type 6 Stout plants with varying leaves (heterophylly) submersed, ribbon-shaped or lanceolate; floating and emergent lanceolate; heart-shaped or arrow-shaped. They are mostly found in the partly emersed phase, but also create paludal types. The emersed leaves and blossoms are on erect stems at a great height above the water.

Biological type 7 Plants which root in the mud, with the roots growing from a stout rootstock. The leaves have long petioles (stems) and they float on the surface of the water. The flowers are on the surface, and the fruits sink after ripening.

Biological type 10 Shore plants, living only in the partly emerged and terrestrial phases. The strong stems tower above the water. They usually have no submersed stage, only the presence of water in their growing medium is important.

Biological type 8 Plants with long stems with leaves, which root in the mud. They are dependent on life in the water, but can, at the same time, have contact with the air (floating leaves, emersed part of the stem and the blossoms). Many aquarium species belong to this type.

Biological type 9 A group of cryptogamous plants—stoneworts (*Nitella*), mosses (*Fontinalis*) and ferns (*Ceratopteris*) of different shapes.

Lilaeopsis brasiliensis. *Lilaeopsis* includes **species distributed in North America, South America, Australia and New Zealand, found on shores or submerged. A type 7 plant.**

Pistia stratiotes **(Water Lettuce),**
see p.22.

1. *Lemna trisulca*, useful in breeding tanks.
2. *Spirodela polyrhiza*, cosmopolitan but not in Africa.
3. *Lemna minor*, see p. 20.
4. *Wolffia arrhiza*, very much reduced in size.

Type 1 Plants

Azolla caroliniana

• DESCRIPTION: A small, usually floating fern, in places growing in the mud, with a short thallus, bifurcated, covered with scaly leaves in two rows. It is only 0.5-1.5 mm long, and the leaves are about 5-7 mm long. Green to red in color, especially in the open; leaf surfaces are translucent and grayish white. They have fine papillary hairs and long threadlike rhizoids on the underside. It is interesting that there are microscopic chains of the alga *Anabaena azollae* living in symbiosis with this plant and fixing the nitrogen there.

Azolla caroliniana

• ECOLOGICAL DATA: A shallow tank of the American tropic and subtropic species is suitable for this small fern. *Eichhornia, Pistia, Salvinia* and *Lemna* can be kept floating in the same tank. It even prospers in wet mud or sand with bog plants and rushes.
• CULTIVATION: *Azolla* does well in shallow water or in mud with *Lemna minor.* A standard aquarium does not prove to be very suitable; a saucer with mud or sand is better and it can be transplanted into the aquarium only from cultures in the open. It has a great need for strong light; insufficiency of light is the reason it often perishes in the aquarium. It hibernates in a warm and light place in the terrestrial phase or in

a damp hothouse. It makes no special demands as to the chemical content of the water; a pH value about 7.0 and a temperature about 65° F. in the winter and 68° to 77° F. in summer are quite sufficient. It is not very useful for the aquarium; it would be more useful to try its cultivation in the terrarium, in damp earth and in shallow pools for tortoises and amphibians. It is very decorative and gives a special charm to the surface.

Salvinia auriculata

• DESCRIPTION: A water fern with oval to egg-shaped floating leaves, 3-4 cm long, with a heart-shaped base and a petiole, without roots. The leaves are flat and covered with fine protective hairs. They possess ternate whorls, two of them floating and the third one submersed (5 cm long) and finely divided and turned into threadlike segments which form the root. There are 4-8 spore-cases on its base.
• ECOLOGICAL DATA: It flourishes with submersed plants both of tropic America and the temperate zone, in pools among water lilies, *Eichhornia* and *Pistia* but it shades the light which would otherwise reach underwater plants. *Salvinia* is also suitable for tanks with large species of *Echinodorus, Sagittaria* and *Nymphaea.*
• CULTIVATION: In nature it grows in stagnant or slowly running water which is clouded with humic matter or with plankton. It does not demand clear water but prefers shallow aquaria with a content of detritus or sufficient sludge and mud. It does not like direct sunshine but prefers a good amount of diffused light, especially in winter. The water should be 65 to 77° F., pH

about neutral with damp air above the water (insured by a cover glass on the tank). Water hardness should fluctuate between 10 and 20 DH. It propagates very quickly by the lateral growth of new leaves, which soon cover the entire surface in a thick layer.

Some species of fish like to hide under growths of *Salvinia* and labyrinth fishes build their bubblenests among the floating tufts. However, the too-dense growths of *Salvinia* overcome other plants in the aquarium; they shade and rob the nourishment from the water in a great measure, reducing the value of this plant to aquarists.

Riccia fluitans (Crystalwort)
● DESCRIPTION: It is an aquatic liverwort. Its body is formed by the thallus which is ribbon-shaped, bifurcated, narrow, linear and fork-shaped. Its color is emerald to deep green. Sometimes *Riccia* forms thick balls on the surface of the water but in the mud it takes a terrestrial form with short rhizoids and anchors itself to the bottom. These rhizoids do not appear in the floating form of the plant.
● ECOLOGICAL DATA: Riccia can be used in breeding tanks for fish fry or to spawn labyrinth fishes, which build the bubbles of their foamy nests under the tufts. They seem to flourish best in tanks with *Cryptocoryne* and *Vallisneria.*
● CULTIVATION: Their water should be soft, mildly acid, pH value 6.8, with a generous amount of light. It flourishes well with good light conditions. The forms growing in bright light or the partly emersed forms have a wider thallus and are brighter green in color; sometimes they are mistaken for other species.

The distance from the light is important especially if the top light falls on the plants. Some parts of the thallus often sink to the bottom of the tank and form very decorative ball-shaped tufts.

Only the terrestrial forms create spore-cases, otherwise *Riccia* propagates vegetatively in the water. It is a very popular and useful floating plant.

Salvinia natans, found in Europe, North Africa and Java.

Salvinia auriculata

19

Duckweeds

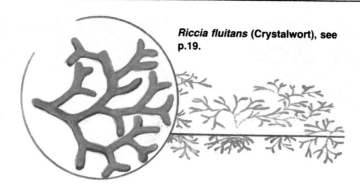

***Riccia fluitans* (Crystalwort), see p.19.**

Duckweeds

This genus (*Lemna*) covers several species of the family systematically related to the family Araceae not by the shape of the body, which is very much reduced, but by the reproductive organs.

These are floating plants often appearing in great quantity; some species even live under water, e.g. *Lemna trisulca.*

The inflorescence is reduced to 1 or 2 stamens and 1 or 2 pistils (monoecious flowers) and a reduced spathe. Most propagation is done vegetatively. The body of the plant usually grows from two round structures similar to leaves which float on the surface and have a root which serves to hold the plant upright.

In nature the duckweeds prefer stagnant water with a great concentration of nitrates and nutrient substances and are typical of the surface water vegetation in village ponds.

In the aquarium they are often introduced by accident, quickly propagating and bringing with them many parasites.

Lemna minor

● DESCRIPTION: A small bright green plant with a diameter of 2-3 mm. It consists of two oval lentil-shaped structures which imitate the shape of a leaf. The root is long, hyaline and colorless with root hairs at the point. Flowers appear rarely in hollows on the sides.

● ECOLOGICAL DATA: Found everywhere as a weed among cultures of water plants. In too great abundance it is detrimental to other species; it robs them of light and nutrients, especially calcium.

● CULTIVATION: It flourishes in clear water, but is known even in peaty waters. It has no special requirements as to light. It is useful as an object of biological observation (cytology). It also serves as a food for some species of fish but is protected from snails by the crystals of calcium oxalate inside the cells.

This plant is rather undesirable in the aquarium, appearing only sporadically. It propagates quickly in a vegetative manner by creating new plants, making carpets on the surface. For the winter it creates turions.

Sometimes we use duckweed for covering shallow water in a tank used as a terrarium for amphibians, turtles, alligators, etc. This plant is injurious to other plants when it covers the surface thickly, and it is necessary at such times to remove it artificially.

Many species of duckweed are used as a green food for

aquarium fishes which feed partially on plants, e.g. livebearers. This food when dried is very convenient in the winter when there is a lack of algae.

Limnobium stoloniferum

● DESCRIPTION: A perennial floating water plant. It grows long trailing runners with rosettes of leaves and long bundles of roots. The leaves are oval, slightly heart-shaped at the base which is covered with hairs and 2-3 cm long. They are green without any spots.

The flowers are bioecious, arranged in threes (3 sepals, 3 petals). The male flowers grow (always 2-3) from the hollow of a spathe. They develop in a natural position only in the sunshine.

Limnobium spongia, a North American species.

● ECOLOGICAL DATA: A very desirable plant in tanks which show the natural surroundings for the Central American livebearers. It flourishes in tanks with spatterdocks, *Myriophyllum brasiliense, M. pinnatum, M. hippuroides, Cabomba, Riccia,* and *Azolla.*
● CULTIVATION: Adequately lighted tanks are suitable, toplight being best while in the littoral phase. Sometimes the roots reach the bottom. For this reason, clay and mud are best in the unwashed sand on the bottom.

Soft water to water of a medium hardness is suitable and the pH should be about neutral. Optimum temperatures of 65 to 77° F.

A well planted and tastefully arranged aquarium. Photo by W. Tomey.

Type 2 Plants

Eichhornia crassipes (Water Hyacinth)

- DESCRIPTION: A perennial, floating, sturdy water plant which has developed a floating structure in the form of aerenchymatous tissue inside of the thickened leaf petiole at the base of the leaf. The leaves create a rosette, pulpy and pea-green in color, 5-15 cm long with many veined nervures. Long roots are in bunches (often 1 meter in length) and form a beautifully colored tangle in the water. They are black and brown with a pink or blue tinge on the side roots. In shallow water, they frequently root.

Inflorescence grows in the middle of the rosette to a height of 15 cm with 5 to 30 blossoms of a light purplish blue color. The petals are fused to form a tube with 6 lobes, 1-3 cm in length. The highest lobe is asymmetrical and broadened with a blue spot. The blossom is similar to that of a hyacinth and the fruit is wrinkled, formed of 3 sections with many seeds.

- ECOLOGICAL DATA: This splendid, interesting plant makes an intriguing addition in a large tank of plants from the American tropics. When introduced into large rivers it sometimes flourishes to such an extent that navigation is impeded. In the aquarium it flourishes for a time. It also can be maintained in outside fish-ponds and garden pools with other plants (*Hydrocleis, Pontederia, Limnobium, Limnocharis*, etc.).

- CULTIVATION: This plant has high requirements as to light, nutritious bottom and the contents of dissolved materials which it draws into its ramified root system. It loves soft water, organic mud with clay on the bottom and plenty of moisture in the air above it. Young plants also are propagated by side offshoots.

It hibernates in mud or in a flowerpot left in a warm place. Not yet frequently used by aquarists but often seen in glasshouses. *Eichhornia crassipes* offers an extensive use to water plant fanciers not only for the beauty of its flowers and its interesting shape in outdoor cultures, but also as a suitable species for aquaria where fish would dig up the bottom, as e.g. cichlids and veiltail goldfish and for the shelter that its roots give to young fish and growing food (mosquito larvae), and so on.

Pistia stratiotes (Water Lettuce)

- DESCRIPTION: A floating water plant with shell-like rosettes of pulpy leaves, light green on the lower side and with a typical grooving and a nervation consisting of 10 nervures. The leaves are spirally arranged around the axis and tongue-shaped (10-20 cm long), narrowed at the base. Covered with tiny trichomes they have a silky velvet luster and are thereby protected from moistening of the surface. Inside the leaves there is an aerenchyma which holds the plant above water level.

The inflorescence is a spadix with a spathe in the hollows of the leaves. In the lower part of the blossoms is the ovary with two stamens growing together. The roots are in the lower part of the leaf base, whitish at first and black and blue in older plants. The entire plant resembles a floating lettuce. It grows stolons, which put out new rosettes.

- ECOLOGICAL DATA: May be cultivated in tropical heated aquaria with some floating plants such as *Ceratopteris, Salvinia, Lemna*, etc.

- CULTIVATION: This is rather difficult, although it is a widespread floating plant in the

Eichhornia crassipes (Water Hyacinth)

tropics. It is difficult to plant in artificial conditions. Permanently moist air above the water's surface (under the glass cover) should be at least 72° F. and the light should be strong. Water drops on the leaves cause brown spots and eventual tissue deterioration. It does not grow well in the aquarium and does better in a glasshouse with a sufficiency of top-light. It prefers soft water, especially rain water, slightly acid (pH 6.5-7.0) to neutral, nutritious bottom with plenty of organic wastes.

Propagates either from shoots or seed. Best way to get it to hibernate is to convert it to a terrestrial form on a damp mixture of sand and peat in a glasshouse atmosphere.

Type 3 Plants

Utricularia vulgaris (Common Bladderwort)

- DESCRIPTION: A perennial water plant. The stalk is 50 to 200 cm long, the leaves are pinnately divided, greenish brown, 1 to 8 cm long and divided into segments which are once or twice again pinnate into hair-like segments bearing utricles.

The inflorescence is a poor raceme with asymmetrical blossoms. Floral stalks are long with bracts in the hollows. The blossoms are a compound of 2 lips and the calyx has 3 lobes. Blossoms are 4 to 15 in number and are composed of 2 sepals and 2 petals with 2 lips and a lower club-shaped spur. They are golden yellow and the borders of the lower lip are bent down. It blooms from June to August. The description of the flower is always important for a taxonomic identification of the *Utricularia* group and as the blossoms appear very rarely there is little known about the distribution of individual species. Very interesting is the shape of the seizing utricles with a valve and hairs on the end. On the upper side of the leaf segments on short stems are utricles 1 to 5 mm in length. Small water crustacea, *Daphnia* and cyclops and others are lured by hairs around the orifice and as soon as they touch the filiform formations, the valve opens and the pressure of water draws the animal into the utricle where it dies and is consumed with the aid of digestive liquid coming from the little glands inside.

- ECOLOGICAL DATA: Found in cold, acid water in association with other species which have the same ecological requirements such as: *Isoëtes lacustris, Eleocharis acicularis, Myriophyllum alterniflorum, Sphagnum cuspidatum* and *Drosera rotundifolia.* It is adaptable to the usual aquarium conditions together with *Vallisneria spiralis* as a good oxygen producer. This fact has been proven by many aquarists.

- CULTIVATION: Bottom with a sufficient quantity of organic mud and peat or with water filtered through peat, giving it an acidity of pH 5.0 to 6.0, without calcium, clean and without algae. In the aquarium bladderwort can be cultivated from winter buds. While it is not suitable for aquaria which house spawnings of small fish, many species of bladderwort would be a suitable object for other experiments and investigation.

Utricularia gibba requires strong light.

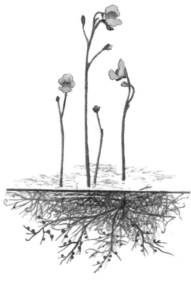

Utricularia exoleta (Dwarf Bladderwort)

- DESCRIPTION: A bladderwort which is much more common in aquaria than the type previously described. Submerged or floating stalks are thin and long, rarely

growing in the mud. The leaves are reduced to small segments, not longer than 1 cm and alternate. Hollow, swollen utricles are not dangerous to fish spawn as in the aquarium they seem to lose the ability to catch small animals. Blooms rarely with white or yellow blossoms on stems above the surface of the water.

- ECOLOGICAL DATA: The bladderwort is appropriate for cultivation in breeding tanks and smaller aquaria used for livebearer delivery. It gets along in association with *Vallisneria, Sagittaria* and *Elodea.*
- CULTIVATION: A very adaptable plant as far as water conditions go. It grows well even in tap water as long as it gets enough light. In winter as well it grows in nice light-green submerged cushions. It grows better in soft, peaty water. Propagates quickly from fragments and by the vegetative growth of the stalk. Cultures of this species must be protected from an overgrowth of algae.

Najas guadalupensis, also known as *N. microdon*, excellent aquarium plant from Central America and southern United States.

Ceratophyllum demersum (Hornwort)

- DESCRIPTION: A submerged plant of 1 to 2 meters in length, with a many-branched bare stalk. The leaves are equipped with small thorns and are very brittle, up to 4-10 forked in whorls.

25

The blossoms have short stems and are sessile in the bract hollows; the fruits are egg-shaped, black, tiny monospermous nutlets. Hibernates and propagates mostly by winter forms, the entire plant showing a distinct seasonal dimorphism.

● ECOLOGICAL DATA: Suitable for the cold-water aquarium together with milfoils, spatterdocks, bladderworts, *Vallisneria spiralis,* with which it does very well, as well as with *Lemna* and *Hydrocharis morsus-ranae.*

● CULTIVATION: A suitable plant for outside tanks or garden pools. It is less suitable for aquarium cultivation because it easily covers itself with mud and sediment, and sometimes even brown algae (diatoms). The stalks are often bare, with only the

Ceratophyllum demersum (Hornwort). Photo by R. Zukal.

vegetative apex remaining thick and emerald green.

A mud bottom is good, or sand with mud and clay, and the water should have a calcium content (10 to 30 DH). *Ceratophyllum* does best at relatively low temperatures (below 65°F).

Najas graminea

● DESCRIPTION: A submerged water plant with a thin, often strongly furcate stem 30 to 50 cm in length. Leaves grow on an axis in false whorls. They are transparent, wide, olive-green, mostly 3 in number, dentate on the sides, 2.5 cm long and 1 mm wide. There are dentate auricles in the hollows of the leaves, and female flowers have 2 pistils. Fruit is about 2 mm long, a one-seed achene.

● ECOLOGICAL DATA: This plant propagates excellently when by itself, where it puts out thick tufts. It is found with species of *Ceratophyllum, Nuphar, Myriophyllum, Chara, Nitella* and *Elodea.*

● CULTIVATION: Cultivation of all species of the genus *Najas* is no great problem. In general we can say that tropical species are ideal aquarium plants, propagating very easily and quickly by cuttings which take root in a sandy bottom. Every segment with several leaves is capable of propagating vegetatively. The lower part of an aquarium bottom should contain about a quarter clay, but they also do well in unwashed river sand and even without sand at all in a breeding tank. It likes a lot of light, which can be provided artificially. *Najas* grows thickly and makes a good bed for the reception of fish eggs and fry.

Temperatures from 74 to 77° F. are suitable, acid water is preferable to alkaline, pH 6.0 to 7.0 and a hardness of 4 to 6 DH.

Type 4 Plants

Acorus gramineus
- DESCRIPTION: A marshy plant, often kept submerged in aquaria with stiff sword-like leaves which often attain 40 cm in length and are 4 to 6 cm wide. They grow in a rosette, are deep green and pointed at the end. They grow from a vigorous rootstock which is horizontal, divisible and about 1 cm thick. The roots grow downwards and on the side of the main rosette of leaves there are additional daughter plants. Inflorescence is a spadix, flowers consist of small, green blossoms.
- ECOLOGICAL DATA: A decorative and hardy plant. Appropriate mainly in the front of the tank, in front of large stones or stumps because it clings to flat stones with grasping roots which grow from the rootstock. *Acorus* goes well with *Cryptocoryne* as well as with *Vallisneria spiralis*, *Limnophila* and *Ceratopteris*.
- CULTIVATION: It prospers well in a light place where the sunshine can fall directly on the front part of the leaves, otherwise it gets stunted. It also does very well in emersed cultivation in a muddy terrarium or on the muddy bank of a garden pool where it frequently grows better than under the water. It can be planted in unwashed sand with clay or a small quantity of garden humus. We have cultivated it in flowerpots. A small amount of dried cow manure works very well as a fertilizer.

Acorus does not place great demands as to water conditions. It does well in neutral to slightly acid water (pH 6.4 to 7.0), and hardness 10 to 25 DH. It prospers in cold-water aquaria at a temperature from 65 to 73° F. It finds trouble getting used to changes in conditions.

Xyris pauciflora, a bog type plant, not compatible with type 4 plants.

27

Isoëtes malinverniana

- DESCRIPTION: From a short rootstock grows a rosette of long, awl-shaped leaves. These rosettes have 10 to 60 leaves each and are 50 to 100 cm long and 2 mm wide. They are light green in color. The upper parts are often transparent, and near the surface are either spirally twisted or float like curly ribbons on the surface. This has a very decorative effect in the aquarium.
- ECOLOGICAL DATA: Is found in lake regions with cold, acid water. With it are *Isoëtes echinospora, I. setacea, I. velata, Vallisneria spiralis, Lobelia* and *Littorella.*
- CULTIVATION: Does fairly well with a sandy bottom with clay added, and the water filtered through peatmoss to make it pure and acid (pH 5.0-7.0) without calcium. Recommended temperature is about 65° F., which even in summer should never exceed 72° F. Does not require a great deal of light, and a mild diffused light is sufficient for this attractive fern. The water should be about 30 inches deep. Propagation is by spores, which can be found at the base of older, withered leaves. They are black and germinate best on a little piece of peatmoss floating in the water. Young ferns are then best transplanted in little pots with peat and clay.

Blyxa echinosperma

- DESCRIPTION: An annual, underwater plant, widely distributed in the tropical zones. Forms a rosette of leaves (as many as 50) which are grassy, tiny, dark green and sharp at the tip. They are about 30 cm long and 0.5 to 1.5 cm wide at the base. Depending on the depth of the water, they can be as long as 1 meter. The middle rib is striking, lateral veins are numerous.

Otherwise the leaves are similar to those of *Stratiotes.*

The long flower stalk is enveloped at the base by a tubular two-lipped sheath which arises from the rosette. The blossom usually consists of only two round green and white petals, with the third one reduced or missing. There are 3 stamens, the ovary has a short stigma.

- ECOLOGICAL DATA: Does well in association with the *Cryptocoryne* species, especially *C. affinis* and *C. becketii.* This is one of the most widely distributed plants of the shallow waters in the rain forest of the lowlands, together with *Nitella* and the *Cryptocoryne* species.
- CULTIVATION: This plant is not common in the aquarium as yet. Good for specialists, as it must be planted every year from seeds. In pure aquarium sand it merely vegetates. Requires a muddy bottom (or a mixture of clay and peat), soft water which is acid (pH 5.3 to 5.9) and a water temperature of 77 to 84° F.

Lighting is important. The best is to use plant lamps to give an intense light, and the water must be shallow. It even sends out shoots in this light.

Eleocharis acicularis (Hair Grass)

- DESCRIPTION: Partly to completely submerged plant, often used in the aquarium in its underwater form. Filiform stalks are in little bunches, in tufts of 2 to 16. They are 5 to 10 cm long, depending on the depth of the water. The stalks grow out of a trailing rootstock which puts out many roots, and each stalk of grass has a tiny bunch of roots beneath. The plants flower only when out of water in damp soil. The blossom is an egg-shaped little spike growing on a quadrangular stem which is sheathlike at the base. Fruits are achenes, glossy yellow and brown and sharply grooved.

● ECOLOGICAL DATA: Typically occurs in places which become periodically very low in water content, where it grows in common with small plants like *Elatine, Peplis portula* and *Limosella aquatica* in inundated river zones or flooded meadows and the shores of ponds and lakes. In the aquarium the underwater form is generally used (*Eleocharis acicularis forma submersa*). The plant combines well with all *Cryptocoryne* species, *Vallisneria spiralis* and *Vallisneria asiatica* in a peaty, rather acid bottom.

Eleocharis acicularis shows up exceptionally well where it is planted by itself. Threadlike axes form a grassy, thick tiny cover similar to green draperies.

● CULTIVATION: An undemanding plant which will require a mixture of unwashed sand as well as plenty of organic detritus or fine mud. The water should be slightly acid. Light

requirements are medium but when too low it is apt to rot. It is green even in winter. Often it takes its time when transplanted in getting used to its new surroundings and water depth.

Eleocharis vivipara

● DESCRIPTION: Perennial bog plant. Down from a long, thin, trailing rootstock there are bundles of roots above which, with the submerged form, there are whorls of new many-branched stalks with adventitious roots on the base. The whorls are easy to divide and are often broken by the current and form a new plant wherever they settle.

Blossoms appear rarely, and only with the terrestrial form. Fruits resemble tiny nuts after they ripen and are gray and triangular.

● ECOLOGICAL DATA: Keeping this plant requires a lot of space on the water surface. *E. vivipara* may be associated with sturdy

Eleocharis acicularis

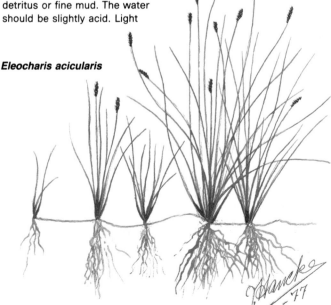

29

species of *Echinodorus* and *Vallisneria.* Although in nature they never appear with the *Cryptocoryne* species, they get along well with them.

• CULTIVATION: A bottom of unwashed river sand with peat and clay is highly recommended for the good growth of this plant. Tap water which is clean and slightly acid is best.

Sagittaria subulata, see p. 32.

Subularia aquatica (Awlwort)

• DESCRIPTION: A small stemless perennial water plant; a tuft of awl-shaped leaves. Flowers minute, white in sparse racemes on erect stems 2-10 cm high. Pistil without style, forming a globular capsule with a few small seeds.

• ECOLOGICAL DATA: Grows underwater in clear cold lakes or sluggish streams, usually on a sandy bottom, exposed on the

shores as the water recedes. *Forma depressa* is especially suitable for small cold-water aquaria in thick tufts with *Callitriche, Elodea canadensis* as well as in special monoculture or in the open.

• CULTIVATION: Small cold-water aquaria with a sandy bottom, clean water and temperatures from 58 to 68° F. but not less than 50° F. in the winter. Water should be neutral or mildly acid (pH 6.5 to 7.0) and the hardness from 10 to 15 DH. It is very rarely used as an aquarium plant.

Arrowheads

The arrowheads (*Sagittaria*) are among the most frequently grown and best-known water plants from the earliest days of the aquarium hobby. They are one of the hardiest and easy to grow water plants in our tanks.

They are similar in general appearance to the submersed leaves of the genus *Echinodorus* and *Vallisneria,* but they differ in the arrangement of their vegetative organs in the blossoms. These blossoms are of one sex only, i.e., they have either the stamen or the pistil in one blossom. The fruits are grouped in a circle and consist of flat achenes. The blossoms are clustered most frequently in ternate whorls in cluster-like inflorescences up to a meter in length. The female blossoms appear below, with the males above. The blossom is arranged in threes: it has 3 green sepals, 3 white petals and an abundance of stamens or pistils. Fruits are achenes with little beaks.

The leaves are highly variable. Under the water they are long, ribbon-shaped or threadlike, with floating leaves being developed later, with the oldest leaves above the water and erect with a strong

Blyxa auberti, most cultivated
plant of its group.

petiole; these leaves are
lanceolate, oval or arrow-shaped
as well. Often all of these leaf
types develop simultaneously on
one plant or they change their
shapes according to water depth,
the amount of nutrition in the
bottom or the lighting
(heterophylly). It seems that the
blue part of the solar spectrum
plays a great part here. The
adaptability to varying conditions
and frequent resulting conditions

Vallisneria natans v. natans

31

Sagittaria graminea v. graminea

cause great taxonomic difficulties with the different species, and only the blossoms and fruits are safe guide-posts.

In nature the arrowheads grow as swamp plants or in flooded areas along the edge of fishponds, pools or in shallow river beds. They prefer sunny places and adapt themselves to the depth of the water and direction of the current, to which they react by turning the leaves (rheotropism). They root in the mud and in deeper water usually form floating leaves. The aquarium species form mostly underwater ribbon-shaped leaves in a rosette. They propagate by shoots, sometimes even by tubercles. They frequently bloom and their seeds germinate quite easily.

The aquarium species of arrowheads make no great demands as to the nature of the bottom. They often thrive where other plants do very poorly, in shady places in the aquarium and in common unwashed sand.

Sagittaria subulata
● DESCRIPTION: Underwater species of arrowhead, greatly variable and adaptable to its conditions and excellent for the aquarium. From a short rootstock appear side runners with young plants growing from them. The leaves are ribbon-shaped and often bent or crooked. Their length ranges from 5 cm to 50 cm according to the depth of the water. The nervation of the leaf consists of three veins, two of which end at the side under the apex of the leaf, while the central one goes clear into the tip. The apex of the leaf is not dentate (in contrast to the very similar leaf of *Vallisneria spiralis*). The inflorescence floats on the water surface. The blossoms are white and bloom for a short time only; the male blossoms have 7-8 yellow stamens. This species is very common in aquaria.
● ECOLOGICAL DATA: *Sagittaria subulata* is a very popular and well-known aquarium plant suitable to be planted in aquaria together with *S. graminea, S. teres, Ludwigia, Myriophyllum, Heteranthera, Azolla, Salvinia* and

32

Vallisneria americana (Val)

Elodea. Suitable for shady, less lighted places or for the background.
● CULTIVATION: Sand with clay, water containing lime (calcium) without any chlorine, preferably smaller tanks or those with a shallow water surface are optimal conditions for this undemanding species. In winter a temperature as low as 62° F. is sufficient, and in summer there should be more sunshine and temperatures between 68 and 78° F. Arrowheads propagate readily by means of shoots; propagation by seeds is not popular with most aquarists. Plant 5 or 6 plants in smaller aquaria in tufts.

Vallisneria americana (Val)

● DESCRIPTION: Underwater plant with strong ribbon-shaped leaves in rosettes up to 1 m long, growing from a rootstock. The leaf nervation is dark red (usually missing in *V. spiralis*). The male blossoms have egg-shaped supporting bracts 1-2.5 mm in length with 3 sepals which separate from the plant and float on the surface of the water when ripe. The female blossoms have supporting bipartite spathes which float with long filiform twisted stems on the water surface. They have 3 sepals, 3 petals and a longitudinal ovary with a trilobate stigma. The fruit is a capsule on a 5-10 cm long stem.
  The biology of blossom pollination with this species is very interesting. When the floating male blossoms come near the female ones, the stamens touch the stigmas of the female blossoms and pollination takes place on the surface. After pollination the female blossoms draw back to the base of the leaves by shortening the spiral stem and the fruits ripen under the water. The fruit is spread further either with the aid of the

Vallisneria natans
v. biwaensis

water current or the birds which live on the fleshy fruit body.
● ECOLOGICAL DATA: In nature this plant frequently appears in brackish waters. Suitable for the kind of aquarium where the fish require a mixture of fresh and sea water or the addition of salt (*Mollienesia*). Other genera such

33

as *Samolus, Ruppia* and others have the same property. Otherwise this plant supplants the common *V. spiralis* in many aquaria.

● CULTIVATION: *Vallisneria americana* is a very hardy aquarium plant with very small demands as to its cultivation. It requires only unwashed river sand with mud in a thin layer and slightly acid water with a pH value of 6.0-7.0. It should have sufficient light, especially direct sunlight and toplight above the aquarium. The water temperature during vegetation should be over 65° F., in the winter about 58° F. Propagates with numerous offshoots.

Vallisneria spiralis

● DESCRIPTION: Perennial dioecious water plant with a short rootstock from which grow rosettes containing 5-20 light green leaves, ribbon-shaped, 20-80 cm long and 5-12 mm wide. The nervation consists of 5 longitudinal veins all of which end parallel to the tip of the leaf (which is different from the underwater leaves of *Sagittaria*). The tip of the leaf has conspicuous tiny dentation which is easily visible under a magnifying glass. The base of the leaf near the rootstock is reddish brown or reddish blue; the very similar leaves of *Sagittaria subulata* have white ends.

Male blossoms of *Vallisneria* are tiny, situated at the base of leaves, wrapped in transparent membranous bracts in the shape of a sac (spathe) and are greatly

Vallisneria gigantea

reduced. They have only 2 stamens and since the entire formation has an air bubble inside, it rises up to the water surface after ripening and floats on dish-shaped hollow petals.

The other plants bear the female blossoms which grow on long, filiform, spirally twisted stems (hence the name *spiralis*, rather than because of the twisted leaves) and are larger than the male ones and more developed. They grow out of a cylindrical green spathe of 2 bracts 1.5 cm long; the ovary is of the same length, petals are fully developed and there are 3 stigmas. The spirally twisted stem grows very quickly, *as much as 2*

Ottelia alismoides, see p.36.

cm in an hour, and takes the ripe female blossom to the water surface where pollination takes place. The blossoms are united by the action of the water current. After pollination the inequality of the two vein bundles causes the spiral to twist more tightly, and thus the ovary is drawn under the water.

The fruit is a cylindrical, indehiscent capsule with many seeds which germinate easily in sand and shallow water.

- ECOLOGICAL DATA: Grows well with the genera *Cryptocoryne, Limnophila* and *Ceratopteris,* as well as *Hygrophila* in Asiatic setups; in African tanks it does well with the *Aponogeton* species and *Ceratopteris thalicroides.* In South American tanks it may be combined with *Cabomba, Myriophyllum, Elodea, Heteranthera* and *Ludwigia* as well as some species of *Echinodorus.*

Some aquaculturists claim that after a time *V. spiralis* does not get along with some species of *Sagittaria,* as these prefer water with a higher content of calcium than is best for *Vallisneria.*

- CULTIVATION: *Vallisneria spiralis* has been an old aquarium favorite for many years. It is an ideal aquarium plant because it can adapt to a wide variety of conditions. It makes no great demands as to the bottom in which it grows and does well even in washed gravel, making it a favorite among beginners as well as veteran plant growers. It gives a tank an authentic appearance and makes an excellent background. It does well with many species of water plants, especially in a deep tank with acid water. Given enough light, especially sunlight, it propagates freely with numerous offshoots.

Ottelia alismoides

- DESCRIPTION: An aquatic plant with two kinds of leaves (heterophylly). The young submersed leaves are ribbon-shaped and broader in the central part and the older ones, which develop later, have a petiole 10-20 cm long; the leaf blade is light green, round and lanceolate, easily breakable, 5-17 cm long and 3-15 cm wide. The leaf tissue among the nervation is often unequal so that the surface of the leaf is bulging and wavy. Leaf borders are lifted and frequently take on a trumpet-like form.

Individual blossoms float on the water surface on stems which grow from hollows in the bipartite bracts and have 3 white or greenish petals 3 cm long. The fruit ripens under the water; it is a round capsule with 6 ridges.

- ECOLOGICAL DATA: It is a delicate plant which lays great claims to the grower's talent. Cultivate it by itself and grow young plants directly from the seeds. When they have put on a little growth, transplant them in tanks together with *Vallisneria spiralis, Eleocharis acicularis* and possibly with *Cryptocoryne.*

- CULTIVATION: A beautiful, very ornamental and rare plant in the aquarium. Requires an experienced grower and is not for the beginner. The plants cultivated from the seeds are transplanted from the flat pots where they germinate into the aquarium bottom consisting of unwashed sand, $1/4$ clay and $1/4$ peat. Suitable water for *Ottelia alismoides* is clear, without chlorine, acid (pH 5.5-6.9) and without calcium. A temperature between 72 and 84° F. is best. When there is enough light the plants even bloom in the tank. They seldom hibernate successfully and usually die in the spring.

*Ottelia ulvifolia,*a species from
West Equatorial Africa,
presumably develops red leaves
also.

Type 5 Plants

Anubias congensis

- DESCRIPTION: Widely lanceolate leaves grow from a horizontal, stout, trailing rootstock, with petioles 25 cm long, the blade 20 cm long and 10 cm wide, with a slightly hairy texture. The leaves are dark green, a little lighter in the back, and have many veins which run to the border.

The inflorescence is of the same length as the leaf petiole and consists, as with *Cryptocoryne,* of a spadix enveloped by a green spathe which is 2.5 to 5 cm wide and 1-2 cm wide. The spadix has tiny blossoms in spirals.

- ECOLOGICAL DATA: Can be kept with *Aponogeton* species, *Ceratopteris thalicroides,* and perhaps with *Vallisneria.* Appears as a swamp plant in tropical rain forests along rivers.
- CULTIVATION: Once acclimated, young plants do well in a sand bottom with a clay content. If possible, the aquarium should be heated at the bottom and kept above 77° F., with soft water that has a great humic acid content. Propagates by rootstock division.

The *Anubias* species are best adapted for terrarium culture where they can grow in a partially emerged state in a heated environment.

Lagenandra ovata

- DESCRIPTION: The genus *Lagenandra* differs from the genus *Cryptocoryne* in the female blossoms, which have pistils in more than one row above the other. A swamp plant which gets to be as high as 90 cm. It has a rootstock which trails in the mud and puts out leaves with striking pointed bracts and petioles which are 45-60 cm long. The leaf blade is elliptical, leathery, 20-45 cm long and 7-12 cm wide and dark green in front, sometimes brownish.

Blossoms grow on a spadix in a spathe which is 30 cm long, purple in color and coming to a point.

- CULTIVATION: Cannot be properly cultivated in an indoor aquarium, but can be kept in hothouses at tropical temperatures with other species of *Lagenandra, Lassia* and the rarer species of the family Araceae, better grown in the emersed or semi-emersed stage. It should have a quite deep layer of nutritious earth, a mixture of leaf-mold and turf, charcoal and river sand. Plenty of light, humid air and temperatures over 73° F. should be provided for its cultivation in a hothouse. Propagates in a vegetative way with the aid of shoots. The rootstock contains a poison.

Crypts

Swamp and water plants of genus *Cryptocoryne* are typical bog plants which have adapted to the amphibian way of life (amphibian plants) in their tropical habitat, due to the rising and sinking of the level of water in bogs, swamps and rice fields. They have stiff leathery leaves which readily withstand high concentrations of humic acid in water. They are undemanding as to light requirements.

They captured the interest of aquarists by their graceful appearance. They are very decorative, especially when artificially lighted, but make certain demands on aquarists.

Their growth is very slow and take a long time to root, often 6 months. Plants often lose their leaves at once. They propagate mostly in a vegetative manner or from a widening of the rootstock. They bloom above water by a spadix surrounded by a spathe like the *Arum* or *Colocasia* species do.

In nature they grow in the tropics of the Old World, from West India to West China, Ceylon, Sunda Islands, Philippine Islands and the entire Indo-Malay Archipelago on to New Guinea.

The aquarium bottom should be 10 cm deep at least and composed of rough, unwashed river sand mixed with clay, peat or loam; a layer of detritus should always be left for nourishment of the roots. The pH value of the water should be about 6.5 and the water must be clear, soft and about 5 DH.

Keeping fishes in the tank to provide detritus should be avoided or there will be settlings on the leaves, which hinders their growth.

When putting in plants leave 10-15 cm between them.

To adjust pH value use phosphoric acid, which is also a good fertilizer, or water which has been filtered through peat. Acid mineral water with a low chloride content is of course advised as well. The aquarium should get plenty of light from above but avoid making it too intense or algae will grow on the leaves.

Cryptocoryne is well adapted to tanks where the temperature never sinks below 68° F. nor rises above 86° F. When the plants lower reduce the level of the water. Growth stops at 58° F. and at 50 to 55° F. the entire upper part of the plant dies. These plants like a warm bottom and heating could be beneficial.

Additional nourishment is necessary and can consist of mineral water diluted 1: 100, tablets for hydroponic culture or organic substances. The lack of nutrients, especially the absence of potassium and phosphorus causes the leaves to turn yellow. A common problem with crypts

is leaf decomposition. The cause may be a physiological disorder but a virus is suspected as well and this disease *may* be contagious to other plants.

In order to promote growth, lower and raise the water level in the aquarium or grow them in a damp glasshouse or low-level terrarium. You can also try enrichment with certain vitamins; a great many fertilizer preparations fill these requirements and their use should be tested.

Cryptocoryne minima, from Malaysia, known for a few years only.

Cryptocoryne affinis
● DESCRIPTION: A plant with emerald-green leaves which are soft, long and lanceolate. They have short petioles with short sheaths and grow from rootstocks which create long runners. *C. affinis* propagates by growing daughter plants from these. On the underside the leaves are carmine or purple in color. The color often appears in younger leaves as spots in the base or in the middle. The point

Spathiphyllum wallisii,
best suited
for terrariums.

Anubias barteri v. nana ▲

Lagenandra praetermissa

Lagenandra praetermissa ▲

of the leaf keeps its green color for a long time. The typical coloring appears only when the leaves are fully developed.

The leaf shape of many *Cryptocoryne* species is very similar and can lead to many mistakes in identifying them. A much more useful tool for the taxonomist is the inflorescence, especially the inner structure. It is much more constant and is not so easily changed by outside influences. Here it consists of a spadix and a spathe. Its conspicuous long tube broadens into spiral purple blossoms.

● ECOLOGICAL DATA: *Cryptocoryne affinis* gets along with most of the other representatives of the Araceae. We often plant it with the species *C. griffithii*, *C. becketii* and *C. nevillii*. It is the fastest growing of all the *Cryptocoryne* species and propagates freely by shoots and the spreading of the rootstock into tufts. It is a very hardy and attractive plant and keeps growing in the aquarium for the longest time even when conditions are marginal. It also grows well with *Acorus gramineus, Eleocharis, Ceratopteris, Hygrophila* and *Limnophila.*

● CULTIVATION: We get the most beautiful specimens by growing them in earthen saucers, flowerpots or glass saucers which contain a nutritious bottom and strengthen the main plant by trimming off lateral shoots. In this way you can achieve fairly nice specimens. If grown by itself, cover the water surface with floating plants.

C. affinis is the hardiest of the *Cryptocoryne* species. It grows well even in unwashed river sand. Put young plants in this medium at once, to acclimate them as early as possible. A fairly strong light is added very gradually, or

the leaves lie down and sometimes even die. It prefers the darker corners of the aquarium.

It is tolerant as to temperature, accepting even 65° F. for a long time. Water should be mildly acid or neutral with a small percentage of calcium ions. It is frequently attacked by *Cryptocoryne* disease, a necrosis of leaf tissues or fouling of the leaves, especially in old water. In such a case it can help to change the water or add several drops of 3% hydrogen peroxide in a weak potassium permanganate solution. The point of the leaf is the first to decay, it then spreads to the base and the petiole. The mesophyll decays away. Phytopathologists should be more interested in these pathological changes, but aquarists can also be of great assistance.

Cryptocoryne balansae

● DESCRIPTION: It is a stout plant with long, narrow, lanceolate leaves which are corrugated and irregularly crispate. They are 40-50 cm long their petioles with a sheath are 4 5 cm long and 1-4 cm wide. They are similar to the leaves of *Aponogeton*, especially *A. undulatus* in shape, but they are long and narrow. The similarity is still more pronounced with the species *C. aponogetifolia.*

The inflorescence is a spadix and spathe, usually 10 cm long, which becomes wide in a purple growth that is folded over several times. The spathe is purple, with red points inside. This species has also been propagated from seeds.

● ECOLOGICAL DATA: May be grown with other *Cryptocoryne* species. For greatest contrast we prefer to plant it with narrow-leaved species like *C. nevillii* which gives a growth near the bottom of small, narrow-leaved

*Cryptocoryne crispatula
= balansae* ▾

Cryptocoryne thwaitesii, grows
well emersed or submersed but
cultivated underwater.

plants and
long leaves reach to the surface or lie on it. Other species which may be combined are *C. axelrodi, C. purpurea, Acorus gramineus* and *Microsorium pteropus.*

- CULTIVATION: Difficulties are sometimes encountered in planting. This species does best in deep tanks and needs a good source of light. In its natural habitat it grows in rivers with a rocky bottom and deep mud, 3-6 feet in depth. These rivers are open to a strong sunshine. When this is the case, the form with red submersed leaves appears as well.

In the aquarium we plant it in a light place in the sand with clay and peat. The tank should be at least 40 cm high. For emersed cultivation choose stout specimens which are planted in flowerpots with the water about 20 cm deep. The first leaves spring up half emersed and under suitable conditions (a hothouse) emersed leaves and flowers develop.

Even though it requires some care at the beginning, this is a beautiful *Cryptocoryne.* Once it gets used to its aquarium it propagates vigorously by putting out lateral shoots.

Cryptocoryne becketii

- DESCRIPTION: Long white roots grow from the trailing rootstock which often gets woody, especially if the bottom is deficient in nutrition. Buds often appear on the rootstock and new shoots grow from them which can be planted. If we sink old parts of the rootstock in shallow water and good light, new plants will quickly put in an appearance.

Leaves grow from the inferior part of the axis; they are elongated, lanceolate, and have a violet petiole. The leaf blade is brownish, more conspicuously brownish-violet on the underside. Contrasted to the other species of *Cryptocoryne,* this species is more brown to reddish-brown in color.

Inflorescence appears only when the plant is emersed. The spathe goes from a tube into a short yellowish green growth, rolled up, lanceolate with a deep violet mouth. The inflorescence usually appears in winter or in early spring when their natural waters would be low.

- ECOLOGICAL DATA: *Cryptocoryne becketii* is hardier than most other species. It can be planted with other species of the same genus like *C. axelrodi, C. wendtii, C. affinis* and *C. nevillii.* Association with *C. griffithii* is not very suitable. Near this plant also place *Hygrophila difformis,* which contrasts well with its bright green color to the tufts of the dark leaves of the *Cryptocoryne* plants. If the tank is in a very light position plant the fern *Ceratopteris thalicroides* where it will give a little of its shade. Groups of the different *Cryptocoryne* species can be separated by a cork rind or stumps.

- CULTIVATION: It prospers best in the aquarium with a bottom that consists of unwashed river sand with a mixture of peat at a ratio of 1:10. Also add a little leaf mold, clay or mud. Plant for emersed cultivation in flowerpots in a glasshouse or in a damp aquarium with a low water level. A slightly higher temperature at the bottom is very suitable.

For emersed culture choose stout plants which are able to withstand the change of physiological conditions. This is best done in January or February. During the spring months the long submerged leaves give way to

Cryptocoryne parva, easily cultivated species from Sri Lanka.

Cryptocoryne ciliata, see p.46.

blunt emersed ones. If other conditions are suitable (such as a sufficiently warm and damp condition of the air) you can also expect an inflorescence.

C. becketii is undemanding as far as light conditions are concerned, and a normal amount of light is accepted. The plant becomes more reddish with the stronger light, and with artificial light the leaves become more elongated. Water should be soft, pH value 6.5 to 7.0, with a slight percentage of calcium. The optimum temperature is about 77° F., but it should be a little higher with emersed cultivation.

Cryptocoryne siamensis

● DESCRIPTION: A species of *Cryptocoryne* which is very similar to *C. griffithii* in the shape of the leaves, except that the leaves are more beautifully colored and from 20 to 25 cm in length. The thin and purplish petioles grow from the woody rootstock which is about 6 mm thick. They are from 10-15 cm long.

The leaf blade is brownish-red along both sides, more conspicuously wine-red on the bottom. It is 7.5 cm long and 4.5 cm wide. The inflorescence is yellow and wrinkled crosswise.

● ECOLOGICAL DATA: Like the similar species *C. griffithii* and *C. grandis* it can be associated with plants like *Limnophila, Acorus gramineus* and *A. pusillus. Hygrophila* may also be grown with this beautiful species.

● CULTIVATION: We plant it like *C. griffithii* in unwashed coarse-grained river sand. We add dried-out clay in balls to the roots at the time the plant grows most vigorously in the summer. The mixture of mud from a river bed and peat is also suitable.

Cryptocoryne siamensis grows well in the middle of the aquarium

in a thick formation, fully surrounded by green plants. It is undemanding as to light, and even sunlight can fall into the tank. The pH value of the water should be from 6.5 to 7.0. In the tank keep the temperature about 78° F..and avoid any great fluctuations.

It is a hardy species and one of the most beautiful of the genus.

Cryptocoryne ciliata

● DESCRIPTION: A stout, high bog plant which occurs rarely in a submersed form. The leaves are 15-40 cm in length and 6-10 cm wide with sheathed petioles. Leaf blade is thick, pulpy, long and lanceolate, bright green on both sides, and round at the base. Nervation of the leaf is different from other species, with 6-10 veins running out of the central rib. The emersed leaves are leathery and bright.

Blossoms are on a spadix in a spathe which is 20-40 cm long and broadened to the shape of a blade, purple inside with a yellowish spot. The border of the spathe is ciliated, hence the name *ciliata.* The cilia are 0.5 cm long. On the pole-shaped spadix there are both male and female flowers. Inflorescence is very beautiful, probably the most beautiful of all *Cryptocoryne* species.

● ECOLOGICAL DATA: *C. ciliata* seems to be more of a bog plant, more suitable for pools and glasshouses in emersed cultivation. In its native waters it often appears in brackish water on shores where there is a mangrove growth. In these places it is a tall plant, attaining a height of 70 cm. In the aquarium it often puts out emersed leaves at once.

In a mud-bottom terrarium it does well in common with the *Spathiphyllum* species, emersed ferns like *Acrotrichium, Polypodium* and other emersed

Cryptocoryne spiralis, adapts to hard water.

Cryptocoryne x willisii ▲
= *nevillii*

47

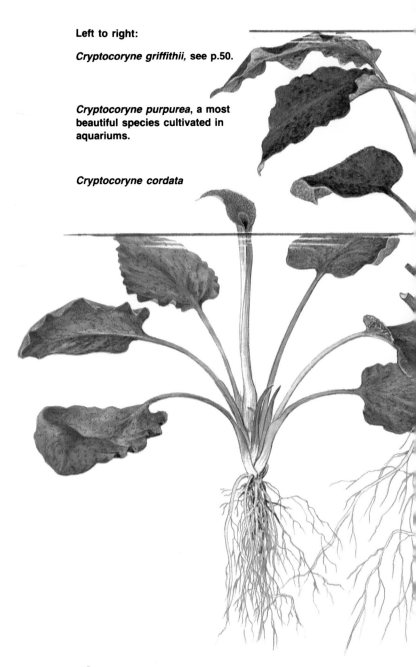

Left to right:

Cryptocoryne griffithii, see p.50.

Cryptocoryne purpurea, a most beautiful species cultivated in aquariums.

Cryptocoryne cordata

Cryptocoryne species.

- CULTIVATION: It does best in a spacious tank with a mud bottom, a terrarium being even better. It is useful in tanks with fish that prefer some salt in the water. It is rather rare.

Its usual method of propagation is by runners, but it can also be grown from seeds. It requires a good deal of light, more than can be provided from an artificial source.

Cryptocoryne griffithii

- DESCRIPTION: A dense tangle of roots grows from a rootstock and numerous lateral sprouts and runners from which *C. griffithii* propagates. Axis is very short, leaves on long petioles which attain a length of 40 cm. They are elliptic to egg-shaped and blunt. On their upper side they are dark emerald green, while the underside is grayish green with a conspicuous projecting purplish nervation. Brown to reddish spots and hollows in the mesophyll often appear, especially if the plant is in a light position.

Flowering takes place quite frequently. The spadix surrounded by the spathe consists of four parts. The lower part is tubular, the middle one ball-shaped and broader and there are male and female flowers inside. The spathe goes to the surface of the water where it opens in a trumpet-shape with an elongated point or even a long growth on the end. It is a dark red. If it does not reach the surface the spathes are shut. Flowers are protected from the water by a leathery flap. The point is spirally rolled. The entire plant is usually 30-40 cm long. Stigma of female flowers is elongated.

- ECOLOGICAL DATA: *C. griffithii* likes to grow isolated from other species of *Cryptocoryne*. When planting tufts it is necessary to leave greater distances (10 to 15 cm) between them. It tolerates *C. affinis* and *C. nevillii*. You can also combine *Acorus gramineus, Vallisneria* and *Limnophila* among stones and stumps in a decorative group and floating species like *Ceratopteris thalicroides* or *Salvinia auriculata* on the surface.

- CULTIVATION: In the aquarium plant in rough river sand with mixture of mud and peat, or use unwashed river sand and water in which peat has been boiled. Flowerpots are suitable for larger specimens. They should have several holes and be filled with a mixture of a gardener's compost (leaf-mold plus loam) and coarse sand. The addition of charcoal proves beneficial as it absorbs gases developed by a microbial decomposition. Simultaneously it controls development of microorganisms which cause clouding of the water.

Fertilizers should be applied in spring months rather than during the rest period in winter. Add pure phosphoric acid (1-2 drops in 10 gallons, mineral water or commercial mixed fertilizers).

Water should be soft; the best is rain water which has been well filtered to eliminate particles of dust, soot and spores of algae. It can contain traces of copper. pH value should be slightly acid (6.5-6.9).

A medium intensity of light, about 12 hours a day with artificial light, should be used. It is necessary to protect plants from too strong sunshine.

Temperature of the water is minimal about 64° F., and the optimal temperature is 78° F. Of course, in their native waters these temperatures are not as important.

Cryptocoryne nevillii

● DESCRIPTION: A perennial plant which often grows amphibiously in nature and is frequently cultivated by aquarists. The leaves are always deep green, 3.5-7 cm long and 1-1.5 cm wide. The leaf blade is linear and egg-shaped, widely wedge-shaped at the base. The leaves can have two forms. The first one is wide (leaves are 1.8-2 cm wide and 4.5-7 cm long), while the second one is narrow (about 1 cm wide and as much as 10 cm long). Nervation is not conspicuous; the leaf is pulpy, leathery and thick. Besides a head nervure there are usually 1 or 2, rarely 3 lateral veins. The petiole is green, 4-5 cm long. The leaves grow from a stout rootstock which is thickly branched. Propagating tubercles often grow on long roots from the rootstock.

Only terrestrial plants get to flower, never the ones grown in the aquarium. The spathe of inflorescence is 5-8 cm long; inside it is warty.

Cryptocoryne nevillii spreads to thick turfy tufts in the aquarium. It may be kept with other *Cryptocoryne* species, especially those which grow high and have a long petiole like *C. griffithii* and *C. becketii*. It fills in the lower parts of the aquarium without reaching the height attained by the other species, and for this reason they do not interfere with each other.

When growing by themselves reduce the water level, and plant it in corners where detritus and other organic wastes pile up. It is a good nourishment for this hardy but beautiful small species of *Cryptocoryne*. It proves to be good in front of rocks, rather than in the back of the aquarium. After a while it covers the tank bottom with a very thick bright green carpet. In contrast to some of the delicate species, diseases are rather rare.

● CULTIVATION: Plant them in unwashed river sand, in hollowed out places where detritus and mud accumulate. A mixture of peat, leaf mold, clay and mud is suitable. Try to avoid transplanting. It takes a long time for a plant to root and get used to its new position.

It propagates by short shoots and tolerates very low temperatures for a long time. It is also undemanding in its water conditions. The pH may range from 6.5 to 8.0, and the water hardness may go to 10 DH. Its extreme hardiness makes it a suitable plant even for beginners.

Cryptocoryne retrospiralis

● DESCRIPTION: This is a stout high plant with long leaves. It grows from a thick rootstock. The leaf petiole is sheathed lengthwise and from 5-10 cm long. It continues in a narrow lanceolate blade which is 15-30 cm long and about 1-1.5 cm wide. The leaf is softly crispate to corrugated and deep green. Where the light is strong it is brown.

The inflorescence is typical and specific, 11-12 cm long. The lower part of the spathe is broadened and it closes up the floral spadix with stamens and pistils; the upper part of the spathe terminates in a spirally rolled up projection (hence the name *retrospiralis*). The spathe is red or purplish inside.

● ECOLOGICAL DATA: This plant can be grown with other *Cryptocoryne* species. A high tank is best and shows off the narrow lanceolate leaves to good advantage. It requires a good amount of light and free room at the surface, and for this reason is not very tolerant of floating

Cryptocoryne retrospiralis, see p.51.

Cryptocoryne albida
= *costata*

52

plants. It is better suited to be combined with narrow turfy tufts of *Cryptocoryne,* like *C. nevillii.* Plant *Vallisneria* and *Hygrophila* with it in an aquarium, sometimes even ferns, *Ceratopteris* and *Microsorium.* These are well tolerated.
- CULTIVATION: When transplanted there is a tendency for the plant to droop its leaves and take a long time to take root and begin to grow again. It is undemanding as to the bottom in which it is planted, and will accept the mixtures used for other *Cryptocoryne* species.

It grows well in the aquarium, but needs a light place which gets a good amount of sunshine. Growth is very slow at first. If flowers are desired, transplant stout specimens into flowerpots in autumn and reduce the water level. The interesting flowers appear rather frequently in January and February. It propagates by dividing the rootstock, but the plant is capable of multiplying by runners as well.

Cryptocoryne wendtii
- DESCRIPTION: The petiole is brownish to reddish, with a sheath which is 12-15 cm long. The leaf blade is elongated, lanceolate, even heart-shaped at the base, colored brownish-green to reddish-green with a dark striping. The leaves are 3-4 cm wide, corrugated to crispate at the edges and 8-10 cm long. In a shady tank another type of leaf is developed, narrow and olive green.

The spathe of inflorescence is brownish-green, up to 8 cm long, broadened into a lanceolate projection which is purple with white warts and a deep violet mouth.
- ECOLOGICAL DATA: A hardy and rather quick-growing species.

Grown by itself it does well, with conspicuous leaves. Plant it in isolation, at a good distance from other species in the lightest spots in the tank. It demands a relatively high water surface. Because of its short shoots, it grows rather thick tufts. It tolerates the presence of *C. nevillii* and *C. griffithii.* With its long leaves it proves to be very decorative.
- CULTIVATION: A bottom in which *Cryptocoryne* species have grown is suitable; add peat, clay or leaf-mold. Otherwise plant it like *C. griffithii* in isolation in a sufficiently light position. It is undemanding as to the composition of the water, tolerating water much richer in calcium ions than most other *Cryptocoryne* species. Optimum temperature for this species is about 76° F., and a sufficiency of light is required, especially from above. A pH value of 6.0 to 7.5, the optimum being about 7.0, is required.

Cryptocoryne axelrodi
- DESCRIPTION: A strong woody rootstock emits many shoots. The leaves, which have brown colored petioles with a sheath up to 18 cm long, grow from it. The leaf is usually 9-12 cm long and 1-3 cm wide. At the base of the blade it is round, with a sharp long point, striped above. The color is olive green. Nervation is deep purple to brown at the base and usually consists of 2 or 3 longitudinal veins and numerous cross veins. The leaves at the water surface are stiffer and deeper green. They are round at the base.

The inflorescence is 11 cm long and 1-2 cm wide (it even widens to 5 cm). The spathe is funnel-shaped and mildly serrate. The spathe is greenish-yellow inside and in the mouth it is bordered with a thin deep green-and-white bordered ring.

Aponogeton crispus,
from Sri Lanka.

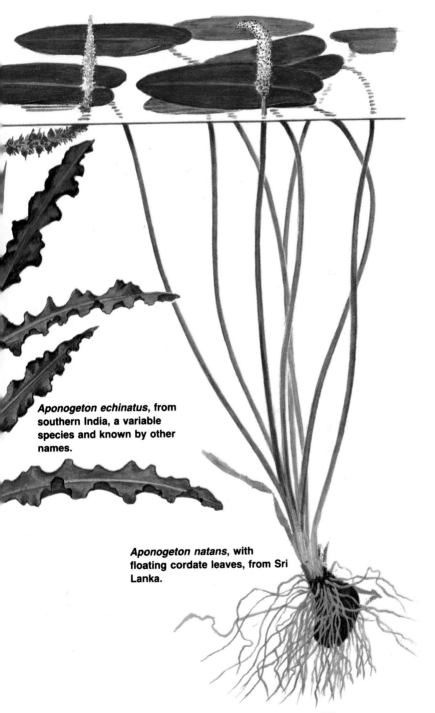

Aponogeton echinatus, from southern India, a variable species and known by other names.

Aponogeton natans, with floating cordate leaves, from Sri Lanka.

55

• ECOLOGICAL DATA: This beautiful *Cryptocoryne* grows best in the middle of the aquarium where there is enough room. In the presence of other *Cryptocoryne* species it only puts out narrow and poorly developed leaves.

It prefers to grow with only its own kind. *Vallisneria* can be used as a background and ferns, especially *Marsilea* and *Ceratopteris thalicroides,* can be planted in front.

• CULTIVATION: Plant it as you would *C. becketii* and *C. griffithii.* It is a very stout species which can even be grown by beginners. Flowers appear only when a nutritious bottom is provided, when the surface of the water is lowered and a damp hothouse atmosphere is provided. Temperatures from 64 to 86° F. are tolerated, and water with a small percentage of lime, soft and a pH value from 6.5 to 7.7.

Aponogeton

The *Aponogeton* species are among the most valuable and beautiful aquarium plants. They have very decorative leaves and nervation, sometimes even bizarrely latticed (*A. madagascariensis*) which is quite unique among all plants. They have a nice flower and propagate only by seeds, putting them in a class which is comparatively rare and difficult for beginners.

Aponogeton bring a characteristic vegetative rhythm from their tropic habitat to our aquarium. They have rest periods when all their leaves fall down. This period conforms to the time of the drought. They also have periods of vegetation and flowers conforming to the rainy season. A tuberous thick rootstock is a main reserve organ and after some time leaves grow from it again, so the care and transplanting of the rootstock is very important. It is necessary to be careful with the flowers, to help the ripening of seeds after insemination in order to expect success in cultivation and propagation. *Aponogeton* are aquatic plants, and they do not develop terrestrial forms.

Their range is Asia, Australia and Africa and especially Madagascar. African species of *Aponogeton* have a two-spiked flower stem, while the others have a one-spiked inflorescence. Flowers usually have a pleasantly sweet odor. They are bisexual, that is they have stamens and pistils, with only two petals and no sepals. Initially the entire inflorescence is covered with a prophylla on the end of a stalk, which falls off after the inflorescence opens. Seeds are modified to be transferred by water and have a spongy cover. They sprout very quickly and in one year attain their full growth. The ecological conditions under which the *Aponogeton* species live are very interesting. First of all they demand soft water without calcium, mildly acid and frequently changed. Rain water is not always sufficiently clean, especially in populated districts, so we dilute the available water with distilled water or water which has been softened by ion-exchangers. The pH value should be 7.0-8.0, hardness 3-5 DH.

Plant the thick tuberous rootstock not too deeply in a mixture of ⅓ rough unwashed sand without any calcium content, ⅓ charcoal, and ⅓ aged clay. It is necessary to add dried balls of clay under the roots during the vegetative period when leaves fully develop. The treatment of the tuberous rootstock is also important when transplanting. It should be soft and not foul, and the softly concave middle should not be fully covered with sand.

Leaves begin to sprout quickly if the water is warm. The tuberous rootstock is given a winter rest period from December to February by trimming off the leaves and letting it hibernate in sand under cold water. If we wish to give fully-grown *Aponogeton* species a rest period, all that we would have to do it to reduce the water temperature to 62 to 64° F. for a time.

The *Aponogeton* group requires a good amount of light,

Aponogeton rigidifolius, a species from Sri Lanka where it grows in deep water (10 to 50 cm).

57

but does not demand direct sunlight. In their native waters they grow in shady parts of rivers and brooks. They do not take very well to artificial light. Most of the species distributed among aquarists at present are hybrids, because these plants cross rather easily. These hybrids are mostly sterile and do not produce flowers but after a while floating leaves start to grow instead. This behavior is almost always a sign of deterioration of a species and of repeated crossing, except of course those species which typically put out floating leaves. If it is possible, get tuberous rootstocks of fresh imports.

Aponogeton bernierianus

● DESCRIPTION: Tuberous thick rootstock, 1-3 cm in diameter; petioles are 5-20 cm long, leaf blade is 20 cm long and 4 cm wide. Leaves are crispate on the outside and are pointed and rounder at the base. Lengthwise nervation consists of one midrib and 2, 3, or 4 lateral veins. Cross nervation consists of numerous veins. Many little windows which consist of fallen-off leaf mesophyll are frequent in places, so that this species creates a morphological interstage to A. madagascariensis where there is no mesophyll between the nervures of old leaves. Irregular squares or elongated interstices arise in this manner.

Hydrotriche hottoniiflora, from Madagascar, perennial in nature.

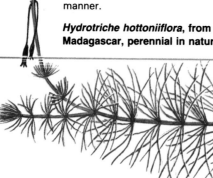

Inflorescence consists of two opposed spikes in groups of 2 or 3, sometimes as much as 6 with white or rosy flowers. Seeds ripen in 10-14 days.
● ECOLOGICAL DATA: This species of Aponogeton is highly tolerant of tropical ferns, Ceratopteris and Leptochilus decurrens, as well as most other African species of Aponogeton, e.g. A. madagascariensis, A. leptostachyus, and A. ulvaceus, all of which demand the same conditions.
● CULTIVATION: Plant selected tuberous rootstocks (cleaned and without old leaves and roots) at the beginning of a vegetative period in February or March in earthen pots or flowerpots, into which there has been put a mixture of sand, clay and charcoal. At first the pots are placed in shallow water 73 to 78° F. Once the sprouted leaves are sufficiently large transplant into a larger aquarium. The plant rests from November to February, at which time the rootstocks may be put out for hibernation or the whole plants be left in water which has been cooled to about 64° F.

This plant is not yet well known and there is a lot to learn about its cultivation. Propagation is rather difficult.

Water should be mildly acid, pH value 6.5-7.0, hardness 4-5 DH; rainwater is best and ⅓ of it should be changed at least once a month.

Aponogeton crispus

● DESCRIPTION: Tuberous thick rootstock is 1-4 cm in diameter, leaves to 30 cm in length, translucent, bright to dark green, 3-5 cm wide. The blades are gently crispate (hence the scientific name crispus), and the petiole is 30-35 cm long. Leaves are round at the base and there are 3-4 lengthwise veins beside the central one.

Inflorescence consists of an emersed spike, 10-15 cm long with white or cream-colored flowers. There are 2 petals (about 4 mm long), 6 stamens, reddish anthers and 3 ovaries.

- ECOLOGICAL DATA: It does well in association with some *Cryptocoryne* species, e.g. *C. nevillii*, *C. becketii* and *C. retrospiralis*. It also gets along with ferns (*Ceratopteris*) and with *Acorus gramineus*. It tolerates other species of *Aponogeton*.
- CULTIVATION: It grows well even in unwashed sand with a slight mixture of clay or mud because it is a species that readily becomes acclimated to aquaria. When it flowers cover the tank with a pane of glass to give the flower above the water enough dampness. Pollinate with a fine brush or with another spike of the same species if several specimens are flowering at the same time. It is rather undemanding in regard to water quality. It accepts even hard water and a greater divergence than other species. Even a hardness of 10 DH is tolerated, and temperatures around 68° F. It blooms in May, June, September and October.

Aponogeton elongatus

- DESCRIPTION: Leaves are very similar to the species *A. crispus*. Petiole is about 10 cm long, leaf blade is 3-4 cm wide and 20-30 cm long and crispate. There are 2-4 length-wise secondary nervures beside the central leaf rib. Leaf base is narrow at the petiole, in contrast to *A. crispus*. Inflorescence consists of a narrow spike with yellowish flowers.
- ECOLOGICAL DATA: Does well with *Vallisneria spiralis*, *Ottelia alismoides*, *Blyxa*,

Ceratophyllum, *Myriophyllum*, and possibly *A. natans*.

- CULTIVATION: Like other species of *Aponogeton*, the vegetative period is during the whole year except from November to February when it hibernates in colder water. This hardy plant is popular among aquarists and is quite undemanding in its water conditions in contrast to some of the other more sensitive species. Water from 3 to 7 DH, pH value from 6.5 to 7.8. *A. elongatus* prefers light that is of a medium intensity, sunshine only occasionally and never for a long time.

Aponogeton madagascariensis

- DESCRIPTION: A tuberous rootstock is 10 cm long, 2 cm wide and cylindrical. A rosette of leaves grows from it. These leaves make this plant a rarity in every botanical garden or collection of water plants. The morphology of the leaves is different. Instead of a normal mesophyll, a lattice full of holes develops. Leaves are dark to brownish-green with petioles 10-20 cm long and an egg-shaped leaf blade, round at the point. It is 15-20 cm long and 8-10 cm wide. There are 5-8 parallel veins with plenty of cross nervures beside the central one. There is absolutely no mesophyll on the leaves, and the whole blade consists of the lattice of nervation like a piece of lace. There is a mesophyll on the youngest leaves.

The inflorescence is 50 cm long and consists of two or three opposed spikes from which the prophylla falls later. The emersed spike is about 5-7 cm above the water. Sometimes seeds ripen even under the water. Formerly called *A. fenestralis*.

- ECOLOGICAL DATA: This plant is too delicate to be placed in a tank with other plants. We must prepare a special tank for it. Its good growth is dependent upon a frequent change of water (without calcium) which is mildly acid, pH 6.8-7.0. Meticulous protection from algae must be given at all times. Floating plants (Salvinia) and ferns (Ceratopteris and Leptochilus) can also be in the tank.
- CULTIVATION: Plant freshly imported tuberous rootstocks without roots and leaves. Put them in saucers with lukewarm water to presprout, after which plant them in a mixture of 1/3 each unwashed sand, clay and charcoal.

The exchange of water is necessary (about 4 DH) for at least a quarter of a tank once a month, possibly more if you notice that the leaves are changing their color. Old water makes the leaves droop.

The use of diffused indirect light is also suitable. This plant comes from the shady banks of rivers and brooks where it gets no direct sunshine; formerly it was grown in botanical gardens in beech casks with rain water in the shade.

Optimal temperatures are 64 to 68° F., so the water should be relatively cold. In a rest period 59° F. or even less is tolerated.

If it flowers propagate from seeds. Sometimes you can succeed by cutting the rootstock, especially if shoots are growing from it. Only patient experts seem successful with this plant.

Aponogeton ulvaceus
- DESCRIPTION: Tuberous rootstock is round, 0.5-3 cm in diameter. Leaves are submersed with a 20-30 cm long petiole. The leaf blade is translucent, bright green, fine, membranous and narrowed at the base. It is 20-50 cm long, 3-10 cm broad, wavy on the sides. There are 2-4 secondary veins, sometimes even 6 running the same way as the central one.

Inflorescence of A. ulvaceus consists of two opposed spikes on a long stalk with yellowish flowers. It is usually about 60 cm long. Flowers have 6 stamens and 3-4 pistils. They appear in May, June, October and November.

A. ulvaceus is a stout plant which demands large tanks. It even reaches a height of 1 meter. Flowers usually grow in soft water and leaves change color according to the hardness of the water, the deeper green leaves indicating harder water. The primary form of A. ulvaceus is rather rare, and most available plants are hybrids.
- ECOLOGICAL DATA: Suitable to be kept with other Aponogeton species and with ferns and Vallisneria. It always requires a good amount of water surface, spreading its fine broad leaves just below. It grows best in a tank with only its own kind.
- CULTIVATION: Plant this species in the same way as other species of Aponogeton and observe its life cycle. In winter cut off the roots and leaves and put it into unwashed sand in flowerpots in cold water for two months in a dark location. After this rest put it back into the tank. A. ulvaceus requires soft, mildly acid water with a rather high percentage of calcium.

When flowering, the floral spike requires a sufficient relative dampness of the air above the water surface and this is why the tanks must be covered with a pane of glass after pollination, or why we put the flowers in a plastic bag. Flowers ripen gradually on every spike, first the lower and then the upper ones. Small seeds ripen after two months and then separate from their spikes and float away. As many as 500 healthy seeds can be expected from one spike.

Aponogeton undulatus
● DESCRIPTION: Tuberous rootstock is round, about 2.5 cm in diameter. Submersed leaves have a petiole 5-10 cm long. Contrasted to *A. crispus* the leaf blade is green, not olive-green to brown, 10-15 cm long and 3-5 cm wide, narrow to the point of the leaf where it gradually becomes the petiole. Leaves are gently crispate and lanceolate and there are two lateral veins on both sides of the leaves beside the central one.

Inflorescence is usually 50 cm long and the flowers are white. When the flowers are ripe you must pollinate 3 times a day. The pollen is yellow and there are about 15 seeds which develop and ripen after a month.

Aponogeton madagascariensis (Madagascar Lace Plant, see p.59).

Aponogeton ulvaceus, see p.60.

Aponogeton undulatus, see p.61.

Aponogeton boivinianus, best grown in deep aquariums.

ECOLOGICAL DATA: It gets along well with *Cryptocoryne* species, but is not sensitive to light. It also tolerates cosmopolitan ferns, *Vallisneria*, other Asiatic *Aponogeton* species like *A. natans* and *A. crispus*, *Limnophila* in single specimens and not tufts, and *Hygrophila difformis*. It is suitable for smaller tanks.

● CULTIVATION: It is a hardy species, popular among aquarists but unfortunately it appears only rarely in its primary form, more as hybrids. It thrives in the usual bottom composition, i.e. in unwashed sand. Temperatures from 63 to 77° F. are quite sufficient.

63

Type 6 Plants

Alisma plantago-aquatica
- DESCRIPTION: A stout bog plant, 10-80 cm high. From a tuberous rootstock the underwater forms grow lanceolate leaves, and terrestrial forms put out heart-shaped ones with long petioles.

The inflorescence of the bog or dry land form is often as much as 1 meter high and the blossoms are small, white or rose, arranged in threes. Submersed leaves are as much as 126 cm long, ribbon-shaped and floating. Older leaves are always submerged.

Acorus gramineus v. pusillus, a dwarf form of a marsh plant that can adapt to aquarium life.

- ECOLOGICAL DATA: Grows together with bog plants such as *Sagittaria sagittifolia, Alisma gramineum, Typha* and *Sparganium.* Suitable for goldfish ponds and pools, also as a bog plant on muddy brook beds and ditches. A very common species in the open.

- CULTIVATION: In a muddy bottom in clay and soil as a stout bog plant. This form does not hold good for the aquarium, but can be used in terraria. It adapts easily.

A similar species, *Alisma gramineum,* is more adapted to water conditions than the above mentioned one, and usually only the points of inflorescence project above the water surface under normal conditions. The submersed form never has fully ribbon-shaped leaves, but more linear to lanceolate. For submersed cultivation in the aquarium you need a sand bottom or plant seeds which have been gathered in nature. These seeds germinate readily in shallow water and young seed plants are more easily acclimated to surroundings in an aquarium than older plants in full vegetative phase.

Luronium natans
- DESCRIPTION: Perennial bog plant with two types of leaves, submersed and floating. From the rootstock grows a rosette of leaves which are up to 50 cm in length. The submersed leaves are ribbon-shaped, sharpened at the tip, 40 cm long and 0.5-1 cm wide. The first floating leaf is oval or egg-shaped, and the leaves further on are egg-shaped and 2.5-3 cm long with petioles 10-70 cm in length and 3 bracts below.

The white blossoms float on the water surface and have stamens and pistils, and in back they are yellowish.
- ECOLOGICAL DATA: Can be kept in cold water tanks in peaty water with *Littorella, Pilularia* and *Lycopodium inundatum.*
- CULTIVATION: Sandy bottom, ⅓ mud and peat added, plenty of light, especially direct sunlight. Can be cultivated all year long in

64

THE WORLD'S LARGEST SELECTION OF PET AND ANIMAL BOOKS

T.F.H. Publications publishes more than 900 books covering many hobby aspects (dogs,

. . . BIRDS . .

. . CATS . . .

. . . ANIMALS . . .

. . . DOGS . .

cats, birds, fish, small animals, etc.), plus books dealing with more purely scientific aspects of the animal world (such as books about fossils, corals, sea shells, whales and octopuses). Whether you are a beginner or an advanced hobbyist you will find exactly what you're looking for among our complete listing of books. For a free catalog fill out the form on the other side of this page and mail it today. All T.F.H. books are recyclable.

. . FISH . . .

Since 1952, *Tropical Fish Hobbyist* has been the source of accurate, up-to-the-minute, and fascinating information on every facet of the aquarium hobby. Join the more than 50,000 devoted readers world-wide who wouldn't miss a single issue.

outdoor pools. It is green even in winter, and in the aquarium *Luronium natans forma submersa* is suitable. Does not blossom and has 20 cm long leaves. *Luronium natans* is an interesting plant, a good object for biological study of leaf shape changes and adaptability.

Sagittaria graminea

● DESCRIPTION: A perennial swamp plant as long as 70 cm. At first tiny ribbon-shaped leaves grow from the rootstock, 2-4 cm wide with 2-4 veins running lengthwise. The emersed leaves have a sheath and a long petiole and are triangular in section. The blade of the emersed leaves is elliptic to lanceolate, narrowed toward the tip. The first leaf is broadened and spoon-shaped.

The cluster-like inflorescence is above water, the blossoms arranged in ternate whorls. There are usually 5-7 in each group. The blossoms are white, on stems, and the female blossoms are more vigorous. They have 3 green sepals and 3 white petals. The male blossoms have many stamens with yellow pollen. The female blossoms in the lower part of the inflorescence have numerous clustered ovaries in a spherical formation. Female blossoms never last more than two days, and the males only one day. After fading the petals with the sepals dry on the stem. The female blossoms bloom earlier than the much more numerous male blossoms. By pollination we achieve ripening and development of seeds. Immediately after pollination the blossoms turn down with the stem. The fruits are achenes in spherical bristly formation, 1.5-2 mm long.

● ECOLOGICAL DATA: This plant requires a rather nutritive bottom.

Sagittaria graminea v. platyphylla, see p.66.

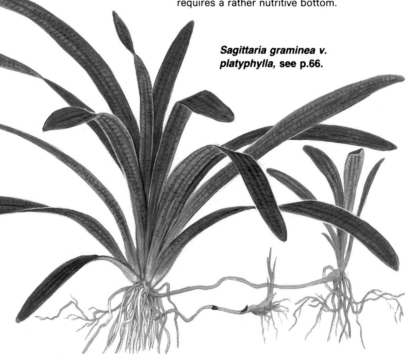

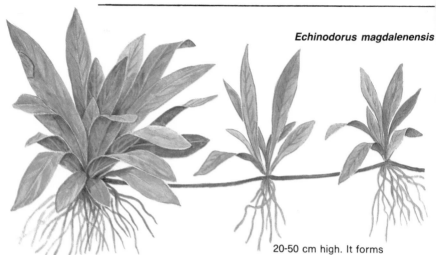

Echinodorus magdalenensis

Plant it together with the other species of arrowheads, water milfoils (*Myriophyllum*), spatterdocks, *Heteranthera, Bacopa, Echinodorus cordifolius* and *Lobelia cardinalis.* All species are planted according to their height, so that they may form characteristic and decorative zones, short species in front and the tall ones on the sides and in the background. The plants with long leafy stalks can grow under the water surface.

• CULTIVATION: Use a rich bottom with coarse river sand, mixed with clay or humus and plenty of calcium and detritus. Plenty of light, especially sunlight, is highly desirable. Under these conditions, if the water surface is dropped in summer, *S. graminea* blooms easily. The ideal temperature is 59 to 67° F., but even lower temperatures are tolerated. The water should be alkaline, pH value 8.0-10.0. The alkalinity can be intensified by adding lime.

This plant is also suitable for garden pools, where it hibernates without any special attention.

Sagittara graminea v. platyphylla
• DESCRIPTION: A swamp plant

20-50 cm high. It forms submerged leaves which are 10-25 cm long and 3 cm wide with 10 veins which run lengthwise. The leaves above water have a petiole 40 cm in length, are sheath-shaped and their blade is oval, egg-shaped and sometimes even heart-shaped. It is *never* arrow-shaped. The usual length is 15 cm and the width 10 cm.

The inflorescence is formed by white, stalky blossoms on stems. It is a medium-sized species of arrowhead, with the submersed leaves very much like other species. Aquarists often call all broad-leaved arrowhead species by this name.

• ECOLOGICAL DATA: A suitable species for both tropical and subtropical aquaria; it associates with *Ludwigia, Elodea* and *Heteranthera* as well as *Bacopa* and *Lobelia.* A suitable species for the community of other arrowheads.

• CULTIVATION: Cultivate them in a similar manner to the other arrowheads.

Samolus valerandi (Green Water Rose, Underwater Rose)
• DESCRIPTION: Amphibious water plant with leaf rosettes consisting of 7-14 leaves at the bottom. The leaves are light

66

green, oval and broadened, 10 cm long and 3-4 cm wide, with a narrow base. Branchy nervation and a whitish color characteristic for this leaf.

The inflorescence is a raceme with tiny white blossoms. The submersed form does not bloom but puts out adventitious shoots.

● ECOLOGICAL DATA: Shallow aquaria are preferred with colder water and combined with *Cardamine lyrata, Sagittaria subulata, S. teres* and *Eleocharis acicularis.*

● CULTIVATION: Plant into shallow water with mud and clay, or as a dry land plant on damp, earthy sand, Water must be soft and clear, with a neutral or slightly acid reaction. *Samolus* often appears in brackish water as well. Temperature should never go above 68° F. and the plant requires a lot of light. As an aquarium plant this species is not yet very well known but is interesting and ornamental, covers the bottom with nice leaves and is suitable for emersed cultivation in soil, too.

Echinodorus

This genus resembles the genus *Sagittaria* by its shape, but all blossoms of *Echinodorus* are bisexual, meaning that stamens and pistils are on the same blossoms. The blossom consists of three green sepals, three white petals, from 6 to 50 stamens and a great quantity of pistils. After ripening, a ball-shaped fruit arises. The fruits are achenes with a little beak, characteristically furrowed. They are spread by water or wind.

The first leaves of some *Echinodorus* form under water in the same manner as with arrowheads. The leaves are long and ribbon-shaped and are not clearly distinguished from one another so that it is very difficult to determine the exact identification of young plants. It is easier to identify mature specimens that have fully developed leaves, especially in emersed culture.

Their blossoms and seeds are very useful distinguishing marks. The inflorescence on a floral stalk does not often develop in the aquarium; the stem bends into the water and young plants spring from it like shoots. This kind of viviparity is the most frequent way of propagating *Echinodorus.*

Most *Echinodorus* plants are hardy water and swamp plants with a strong root and a perennial rootstock in the mud. At the time of the rains in the tropics some species develop submersed forms with ribbon-shaped leaves

Echinodorus tenellus,
see p.77.

of different shapes on one specimen (heterophylly). It most frequently blooms and grows fruits when the weather is dry.

These plants are very suitable for aquarium use; they are hardy and popular. Above all they may be used for big biotopical aquaria which are used to display the different species of plants and fish found in the American tropics. They grow well at temperatures from 64 to 77° F. A vegetative rest is important, conforming to the climate of their habitat. This means that they rest in a winter season from December to April, at which time they may even throw off their leaves. At this time reduce their temperature without transplanting them.

These plants are only slightly demanding as to water conditions; a neutral water is suitable, with a hardness of 4-10 DH. Add a little clay, clayey earth or even non-acid peat moss to the unwashed sand to form a bottom. The height of these plants, their rank growth and formation of leaves above the water surface, are a disadvantage. To keep them in a submerged state and take advantage of their decorative leaves below the water surface, either cut off the older leaves until a rosette of 6-8 leaves remains, transplant them more often or draw the roots from the sand a little. Another way is to plant them in small flowerpots or in a small plastic bag filled with unwashed river sand. Specialists prefer to

Echinodorus berteroi

plant younger plants in this way and have kept them this way for as much as several years.

Give them a very intense light. Natural sunshine is the best. With artificial light choose an intensity of 8000 to 10,000 lumens. If no runners or shoots sprout, grow them from achenes, planted in shallow saucers with damp sand and a temperature of 77° F. at least and intense light. After germination transplant higher plants into shallow aquaria. This method of propagating by achenes is not very common among aquarists, so instead make wood or metal covers above the surface of the water in big tanks in which *Echinodorus* are kept. It makes a sort of miniature hothouse, which can also be covered with glass or a sheet of plastic. In this way mature plants bloom well and form achenes which will ripen. This creation of a damp glass-house atmosphere will prove to be very successful.

Echinodorus berteroi

DESCRIPTION: A species of *Echinodorus* with very variable leaves of three types. The youngest leaves are ribbon-shaped, linear with a blunt point. Older leaves are 25 cm long and often about 3 cm wide. The base of the blade is round to semi-heart-shaped, with 1-3 lengthwise veins beside the central one. The dark green cross-veins create a conspicuous venation. The oldest leaves reach the water surface. They are wide, oval, egg-shaped, tubular at the base of the petiole. The petioles are as much as 80 cm long. The leaf blade is 10-12 cm long and 8 cm wide.

The inflorescence reaches up as high as 1.5 m and consists of 3 branches in whorls, each with 6 flowers. Floral stalks are pointed with bracts on the axis. There are 12 stamens, a lot of fruits which after ripening create a ball-shaped formation. Achenes are 2.5-3 mm long and have two furrows bent at an angle and three unbent furrows and an awl-shaped little beak.

This is a very beautiful aquarium plant as long as the leaves remain in the first or second stage and there are no large floating leaves on the surface.

● ECOLOGICAL DATA: It is suitable to combine *E. berteroi* with the species *E. cordifolius, E. brevipedicellatus* in big tanks as well as with arrowheads and *Vallisneria* which are usually planted in the background or on the sides of the tank. Plant *E. tenellus, E. intermedius, Sagittaria eatonii* and other plants which form turfy carpets as a lower layer at the bottom of the tank. It is also suitable to introduce floating plants like *Lemna, Riccia* and *Azolla* which shade the tank and hinder the formation of surface leaves.

● CULTIVATION: Mix the bottom out of sand, a quarter of which is mixed with clay and peat. Acid water is better than alkaline with a calcium content, a pH value of 6.8-7.0 is the most suitable. The best temperature is 68 to 76° F. Depth of the water should be 40-50 cm. *E. berteroi* does not put out vegetative lateral runners and only sporadically accidental are new plants put out from the mother tuft. It is well to drop the temperature in winter and let the plant undergo a rest period; at this time it even sheds the lower leaves.

Propagate *E. berteroi* by taking cuttings from its rootstock, but the usual way is by planting seeds. It is not a very suitable species for a home aquarium

Echinodorus horemanii, easy to grow and also decorative. ▼

Echinodorus palaefolius v. latifolius ▼

▲
Echinodorus ovalis = horizontalis

70

Echinodorus subalatus, from
Central America to Brazil.

Echinodorus
cordifolius, see
p.72.

because it often develops floating and emersed leaves. It does well in swampy aquariums or terrariums because of its inclination to grow amphibiously.

Echinodorus brevipedicellatus (Small-leaved Amazon Swordplant)

● DESCRIPTION: A perennial plant, usually only submerged in the aquarium. The leaves form a rosette and they grow from only a short rootstock. The green leaves are 25-55 cm long and their petioles are 5-15 cm long; the leaf blade is very narrowly pointed. They are often bent with a middle rib standing out. Alongside, 2-4 pairs of lateral veins stand out, one from a main vein in a lower third and the other converging to the leaf base.

The inflorescence is usually 1 m long and consists of 4-6 small whorls with little white flowers. Bisexual flowers (those that have stamens and pistils) contain 12 stamens and many ovaries inside. Fruits are 3-4 mm long with 8 furrows and they develop only as terrestrial forms. In the aquarium flowers are usually substituted by young plants which grow on stalks under the water.

● ECOLOGICAL DATA: *Echinodorus brevipedicellatus* requires a spacious tank with a capacity of at least 20 gallons. It does very well when kept in a tank with no other species. In fertile tanks it grows with water milfoils, especially with the species *Myriophyllum brasiliense* and *M. Heterophyllum*. It also tolerates the presence of some other species of *Echinodorus*, *Vallisneria spiralis*, *Potamogeton gayi* and *Ceratopteris thalicroides*.

● CULTIVATION: Plant it in the usual aquarium bottom with a deep layer of unwashed sand. The second year after they have become acclimated to their new medium, when the nutriments are becoming depleted, we add clay balls which have been mixed with river mud and dried.

If the plant attains maturity and has seeds and fruit you can even plant the seeds and grow them.

Young plants usually develop on a long stem and are held down to the bottom with stones or little plant weights. Only after it takes root do we cut off the primary floral stem. If this is done too soon, the young plants often rot.

E. brevipedicellatus requires a rather large amount of light, but is not very choosy when it comes to water conditions. The pH value may lie between 6.0 and 7.0, and the hardness between 5 to 12 DH Temperatures should not be lower than 65° F. A higher percentage of calcium does not matter, but it often causes an incrustation on the leaves of calcium carbonate as a result of the intensive assimilation.

This species is very popular among aquarists, who favor it because it never produces floating or emersed leaves.

Echinodorus cordifolius

● DESCRIPTION: A high, stout water or swamp plant with heart shaped leaves (giving us the name *cordifolius*). Leaves are widely oval at first, 10-20 cm long and 6-10 cm wide. As they grow they are heart-shaped at the base, bluntly pointed and have 2-4 central veins which run lengthwise and continue as far as the leaf base. The petiole is 5-15 cm long, and on the emersed leaves even 50-75 cm long.

The rootstock is tuberously thick, with richly branched roots. On the leaves there are brownish translucent spots, 1-3 mm long, scattered on the blades. After some time emersed leaves are formed which are very much

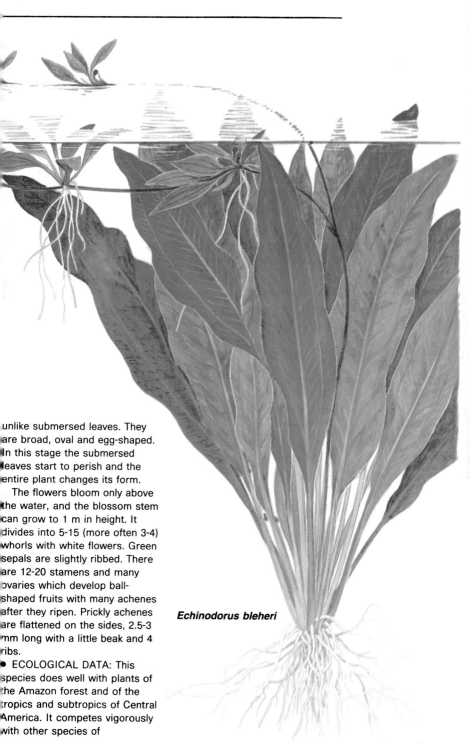

unlike submersed leaves. They are broad, oval and egg-shaped. In this stage the submersed leaves start to perish and the entire plant changes its form.

The flowers bloom only above the water, and the blossom stem can grow to 1 m in height. It divides into 5-15 (more often 3-4) whorls with white flowers. Green sepals are slightly ribbed. There are 12-20 stamens and many ovaries which develop ball-shaped fruits with many achenes after they ripen. Prickly achenes are flattened on the sides, 2.5-3 mm long with a little beak and 4 ribs.

● ECOLOGICAL DATA: This species does well with plants of the Amazon forest and of the tropics and subtropics of Central America. It competes vigorously with other species of

Echinodorus bleheri

Echinodorus argentinensis

Echinodorus. If it is smaller and not fully developed, it tolerates *E. intermedius, E. brevipedicellatus, E. argentinensis* and *E. maior*, all in the same tank. Up to about 10 cm away plant tufts of *Vallisneria gigantea, Elodea* and *Heteranthera.*

● CULTIVATION: The use of unwashed sand and trimming the rank growth above the water will keep this beautiful species with conspicuous softly green underwater leaves for a long time. The depth of the water does not have any great influence on the formation of emersed leaves.

The mixture of a clay and mud hastens the formation of blossoms during the time of optimal development in the summer. Also there are daughter offshoots alongside the mother plant. Sometimes you can rejuvenate an old plant by cutting off all leaves at the base of the petiole without destroying the plant. Of course, this should be done only in the summer when new shoots come very easily.

E. cordifolius propagates frequently by shoots in the hollows of buds on the floral stalk but more often from the seeds after the blossoms are shed.

Temperature from 68 to 76° F. is suitable for this species, with light of a medium intensity. Natural sunlight is preferred. With artificial light the leaves become pale and the plants often lose their leaves after transplanting.

Neutral water is suitable, and a hardness up to 14 DH is tolerated.

Echinodorus argentinensis

● DESCRIPTION: *E. argentinensis* is a stout plant for larger tanks. It is very decorative. Leaves are olive to dark green, elliptic to oval. They are 15-25 cm long and about 10 cm wide. There are 5-7 veins which converge at the point and at the leaf base. The leaf

Echinodorus macrophyllus, large species, requires a big tank.

petiole can get as long as 50 cm, and leaves often grow above the water, even in deep tanks.

- ECOLOGICAL DATA: This species is suitable for large aquaria and we usually plant it in the middle because it is a large plant. It tolerates the presence of other large species of *Echinodorus, Cabomba, Elodea* and *Myriophyllum. Echinodorus tenellus* and *E. intermedius* are suitable for foreground plants.
- CULTIVATION: It grows and propagates well in a deep layer of unwashed river sand to which has been added some clay and a little good garden earth (mixed leaf-mold and peat). The plant demands this nutritious substance especially in the second year. It requires a goodly amount of light, preferring sunlight of sufficient intensity, preferably from the southeast. Temperature 66 to 77° F., neutral water about 9-12 DH are best, with other conditions similar to those given to other large *Echinodorus* species.

Blossoms appear most often in a glasshouse or under the cover of a tank which gets a lot of illumination.

Propagating this plant in a vegetative manner is very difficult because it does not produce runners. It is only possible to divide the mother tuft of leaves by cutting the rootstock. Always sprinkle the cut section with charcoal to forestall rotting. It is most often propagated from seeds.

Echinodorus latifolius (Dwarf Amazon Swordplant)
- DESCRIPTION: A perennial water or shore plant which grows a rosette of leaves and plenty of shoots. Submersed leaves are narrow, lanceolate and sharp, sometimes oval. Leaf blades are bright green, up to 15 cm long and 1-4 cm wide. The central vein is a darker green, and beside it there are three or more lateral veins, but they are weaker and are barely noticeable. Cross nervation is thick. Petiole is up to 20 cm long. Leaves of emersed forms grown in mud are lanceolate and their blade is 3.5 cm long and 1 cm wide.

Inflorescence is an umbel about 30 cm high with 4-7 white flowers on high stalks with bracts. The fruit is an oval achene 1.5-2 mm long with 6-8 furrows and a little beak. Flowers do not grow under water but the plant always puts out plenty of runners so it propagates very quickly at regular distances, probably more so than any other aquarium plant.

- ECOLOGICAL DATA: The plant is suitable for heated aquaria. It flourishes in common with the similar species *E. intermedius* as well as with arrowheads (*Sagittaria subulata, S. engelmannia, S. terres*), *Echinodorus tenellus* and the American species of milfoils, especially *Myriophyllum brasiliense*. This species is suitable as a low plant in front.
- CULTIVATION: Plant it in a sand bottom in unwashed sand with a mud and clay mixture. It is an ideal plant for beginners, growing under nearly all conditions. In the light and half-shade it creates turfy carpets.

Water should be about neutral, and a hardness of more than 10 DH does no harm. It prefers a higher temperature, 74 to 77° F.

Depending on the intensity of the light, the plant grows two types of leaves. In bright light they are short and egg-shaped, while in shaded spots they are longer and narrowly lanceolate.

Echinodorus osiris, with broad
leaves (right) when transplanted
under water.

Echinodorus tenellus

● DESCRIPTION: A small aquatic
or swamp plant which forms low
rosettes of small leaves which
continue to propagate laterally by
thready runners. Leaves are not
longer than 10 cm and about 2
mm wide, linear, sometimes
narrowly lanceolate with 1-3
veins. A terrestrial swamp form
has stronger and darker leaves.

Inflorescence appears only with
the emersed form; it is usually 3-
10 cm high with one whorl and 3-

77

6 flowers on stalks pointed by three lanceolate bracts. Flowers are 1 cm in diameter. Sepals are egg-shaped, petals are white with 9 stamens and 12-15 ovaries. Fruit is an achene with three furrows and a beak-shaped growth.

• ECOLOGICAL DATA: In the tropics it grows as a perennial plant, while in the temperate zones as an annual one. It grows in wet sand along the shores of pools and in the inundated zones of rivers. It rarely grows in flowing water. A hardy aquarium plant, it forms thick carpets in the sand under water. It is suitable for the tank foreground.

It grows in common with *Sagittaria subulata, S. teres, Lobelia, Myriophyllum, Micranthemum* and some other species of *Echinodorus*.

• CULTIVATION: Plant *E. tenellus* in a damp fine sand which contains dried clay, a good quantity of mud, and a great part of peat-moss. Otherwise it grows well in shallow tanks where there is a lot of detritus on the bottom. Reduce the water level to a minimum before it roots. Later it is possible to bring up the water level. To plant fine plants weigh them down with small stones to prevent the plant from floating. Temperature is kept from 64 to 78° F. The plant demands a good amount of light. Hardness of the water should average about 9 DH, pH value 7.0-8.0.

Echinodorus maior

• DESCRIPTION: A water plant which in nature is more paludal and attains a height up to 70 cm. It has a stout rootstock which roots it firmly in the mud. Leaves are 30-50 cm long, lanceolate to ribbon-shaped, corrugated to crispate on the edges and up to 10 cm wide. The color is a fresh green, becoming darker as the plant gets older. They are narrow at the base and continue in a round petiole. The central veining of the leaf is fully developed and beside it there are 4-8 lateral veins which go to the point of the leaf. Two of them start from the lower part of the blade, and the others from the leaf base.

The inflorescence is conspicuously high, attaining 130 cm. Flowers grow in the hollows of bracts which are conspicuously long and pointed. They are about 1 cm in diameter and have short stems. They consist of three green sepals and three white petals, six yellow stamens and 15-20 green ovaries. Fruits ripen after the flower is pollinated and are 2 mm long with a tiny beak and 6-8 ribs. Seeds germinate without difficulty even if planted in a saucer with damp sand.

• ECOLOGICAL DATA: With this species of *Echinodorus* you can add *Echinodorus paniculatus, Myriophyllum brasiliense, Vallisneria americana* and *V. spiralis*. It prospers best when kept in small groups of its own kind.

• CULTIVATION: The most suitable bottom for growing *E. maior* is a rough river sand with a light mixture of mud. A water hardness of 12 DH and a pH value about neutral (7.0) is quite sufficient. *E. maior* does not have a very great tolerance for acid water; it dwarfs. A water temperature of 72 to 75° F. is optimal.

Echinodorus paniculatus (Amazon Swordplant)

• DESCRIPTION: A high, perennial water plant. It has a short rootstock and a rosette of large leaves about 30-70 cm long growing from it. Leaf petioles are three-edged, narrow and 10-30

Echinodorus maior

cm long. The leaf blade is bright green, 25-45 cm long, translucent, pointed at the end and wide in the middle. Venation consists of a midrib and 2 or 3 secondary veins which border the leaf. They are curved and go from the base to the point of the leaf. There are many cross-veins. The venation is different from that of *E. brevipedicellatus,* but in other ways the leaves of both are very similar.

Nymphaea zenkeri

Nymphaea zenkeri, first collected in the Cameroons, West Africa.

Barclaya longifolia, see p.84.

Echinodorus paniculatus (Amazon Swordplant)

The inflorescence can grow to 1.5-2 m in length and produce 5-8 whorls with 6-8 flowers on stalks above the water. There are 10-24 stamens and a lot of ovaries. Fruit is 2 mm in diameter with 6-8 ribs and a small beak. Flowers appear only rarely in the aquarium, where the plants propagate by occasional offshoots. *E. paniculatus var. dubius* has leathery egg-shaped leaves covered with star-shaped hairs on the point of the petioles and at the base of the blade.

● ECOLOGICAL DATA: Add *E. maior, E. tenellus* or *Myriophyllum brasiliense* to this hardy aquarium plant in a large decorative tank. But the best results are attained if kept by themselves, especially in a large tank.

● CULTIVATION: We plant this attractive species in an aquarium with a deep and nutritious bottom, perhaps in flowerpots with rough sand, clay or peat in a light place. After two or three years transplant into a new mixture, and according to the condition of the plant divide the healthy specimens into two or three pieces and then plant these by themselves. Water hardness should be about medium, with a pH value close to neutral. Temperature in the winter should not drop below 65° F., and in the summer 72 to 74° F. is optimum.

If conditions do not suit it, the plant will keep losing its lower leaves. New leaves grow very weak, often with holes in the mesophyll from the lack of nutriments.

Echinodorus paniculatus = bleheri (Amazon Swordplant)

Nuphar japonica, called Japanese Pond Lily; two other varieties of this species are known.

Type 7 Plants

Barclaya longifolia

- DESCRIPTION: From a spherical rootstock grow long, narrow leaves which at first are narrow and lanceolate, later oblong and arrow-shaped, red and green with a transparent bluish shade. They are often corrugated and their venation is red and brown; they are as much as 30 cm long, 3-4 cm wide and have a short petiole about 10 cm long. The leaves are very soft and fragile, green on the back side.

  Blossoms are about 2 cm long with greenish petals and purple to red inside. They differ from the genus *Nymphaea* in the petals as they are placed on the ovary. The fruit ripens under water, and when the capsule opens little hairy seeds fall out and immediately germinate.
- ECOLOGICAL DATA: This beautiful tropical water lily finds its place in decorative tanks with the *Cryptocoryne* species, *Microsorium pteropus* or *Ceratopteris*. In aquaria it represents a rare novelty.
- CULTIVATION: An extremely ornamental species. It does well in the same mixture for exacting species like *Aponogeton:* $\frac{1}{3}$ coarse river sand with a very low calcium content, $\frac{1}{3}$ charcoal and $\frac{1}{3}$ clay which has been well dried in the sun. Water should be soft, 4-8 DH, acid with a pH value 6.0 to 7.0. This water lily has high temperature requirements and does not like the temperature dropping below 77° F. Heating the tank bottom is very good. The seeds germinate best in the same type of bottom used for the mature plants.

Brasenia schreberi

- DESCRIPTION: Water plant with articulated trailing rootstock and floating leaves covered with a slight layer of slime on the parts under water. Round, shield-like leaves float on the water surface and have long petioles. The leaf blade is 3-6 cm long, dark olive-green in front, and at the edges and behind reddish.

  Purplish colored blossoms are about 2-2.5 cm wide with 3 narrow threadlike sepals, 3 petals, 12-18 stamens and 16 ovaries. The fruit is longitudinal and dilated at both tips.
- ECOLOGICAL DATA: *Brasenia* is suitable for small aquaria with water 10-20 cm in height, and less suitable for big tropical aquaria. In summer we can even cultivate it outdoors, but of course it does better under glass with other water lily species, *Hydrocleis nymphaeoides*, *Neptunia oleracea* and *Nelumbo*.

84

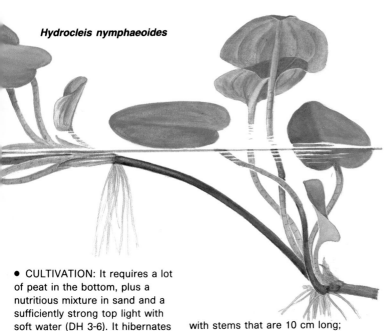

Hydrocleis nymphaeoides

● CULTIVATION: It requires a lot of peat in the bottom, plus a nutritious mixture in sand and a sufficiently strong top light with soft water (DH 3-6). It hibernates with the temperature around 65° F., but there are local forms from northern regions which are hardier.

Hydrocleis nymphaeoides

● DESCRIPTION: Perennial water plant with floating leaves which grow from a rootstock. The leaves are dark green, heart-shaped and egg-shaped, leathery pulpy and light green in back, with a long petiole and a blade 10 cm in length and 7 cm wide. The stalk branches very richly and is about 1 m long, with many shoots that root in the nodes. We can divide these nodes and propagate it by cuttings. Everywhere in the tissues of leaves and stalks there are aerenchymatic tissues that cause corms to float on the water surface or protrude above water and cover the surface thickly.

The blossoms are quite large and very beautiful. They have a shining yellow color with a red and brown center, 4-5 cm wide, with stems that are 10 cm long; the 3 green sepals are not deciduous, have 3 yellow petals and 20 stamens and ovaries that connect at the base.

● CULTIVATION: Although it grows well in the usual bottom where unwashed river sand and detritus prevail, we improve it a bit in the tank by adding clay or earth, and we plant it where there is sunlight as well. It does well in soft, acid water although it is not an essential as it grows well in neutral tap water also. It hibernates in lower temperatures (around 64° F.) and for cultivation a temperature of 68 to 77° F. is quite suitable.

It deserves the attention of aquarists by its beautiful and ornamental appearance and lovely striking blossoms. It is also a favorite plant in tropical hothouses where it is grown with water lilies and lotus. It is also suitable in pools with gigantic water lilies like *Victoria regia* and *V. cruziana*.

Nuphar lutea

Nuphar lutea
- DESCRIPTION: Roots grow down and leaves up from a stout rootstock up to 2 m long and 10 cm thick which has scars from leaves falling off. The first leaves are submerged, translucent, alternate, deeply heart-shaped at the base (10-30 cm long), leathery, oval to roundly elliptic, crispate on stiff flexible petioles. Stoma (air vents) on leaves are on the outside. The next leaves reach to the surface; they are emersed and floating, flat, strong and more pointed.

The blossom is yellow and about 5 cm in diameter. It is cyclically arranged in spirals around the ovary. There are plenty of stamens around the ovary, 5 yellow sepals, numerous petals which are one-third larger, concavely bent and consisting of many tongue-shaped leaves; there are many upper ovaries. The flowers have an odor like an apple.

The fruit is bottle-shaped, pulpy, 6 cm long and 5 cm wide.
- ECOLOGICAL DATA: Typical and dominant species of lakes with a high calcium content in the lowlands and warmer regions of Europe. It appears to a lesser degree in ponds only when they are connected with canals. It creates characteristic associations with *Myriophyllum verticillatum, Ceratophyllum demersum* and *Hydrocharis morsus-ranae.* It prefers sluggish streams and open deeper waters.

In the aquarium in its submersed form, it tolerates the *Myriophyllum* species, *Sagittaria subulata, S. graminea, Elodea, Cabomba* and *Heteranthera.*
- CULTIVATION: Plant them in sand only to keep them in a submerged state. In this way leaves stay submerged even for several years at times and the plant grows well in winter with artificial lighting. It makes some demands as to light. Use soft and mildly acid water, giving them opposite of what they would get under natural conditions and thereby preventing the development of floating leaves. You can find these "starved" forms in peaty waters and strongly shaded river tributaries, and they are very suitable for the aquarium. For aquarium culture plant seeds which are gathered in the autumn. Young plants spring up in swampy sand in the spring, and later these can be transplanted into the aquarium with a low water level. It has no special demands as to temperature.

Nymphaea alba (White Water Lily)
- DESCRIPTION: Perennial water plant with trailing stout rootstock to 1 m in length. Leaves have long petioles with the blades floating

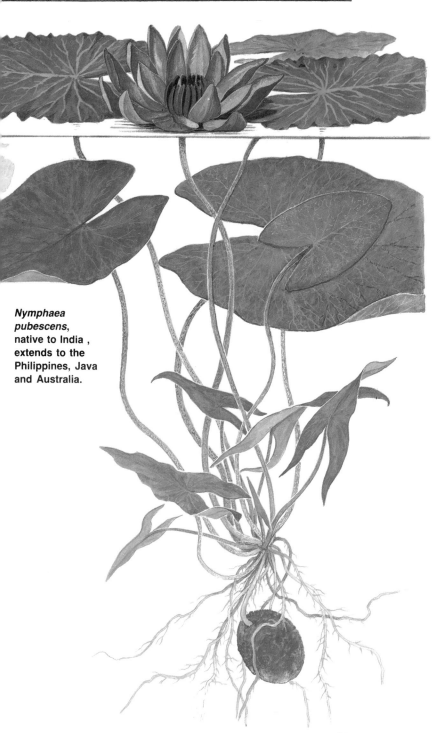

Nymphaea pubescens, native to India, extends to the Philippines, Java and Australia.

or emersed, leathery, egg-shaped, round, smooth-edged, narrowly heart-shaped at the base with opening blunt to cut-off holes, pointed inside. Leaves are dark green, red in places and 9-12 cm wide.

The white flowers are really beautiful, floating on the surface and closing up at night. They consist of 4 green sepals and 14-44 white petals with changeable stamens which are cyclically arranged on the ovary. The stigma has 9-22 rays and the capsule is ball-shaped.

● ECOLOGICAL DATA: White water lilies create isolated and often limited associations in stagnant and sluggish waters; in pools they are found with spatterdocks and water milfoils.

Hydrocotyle vulgaris = verticillata (Water Pennywort), see p. 90. Photo by R. Zukal.

Stratiotes and *Trapa,* and possibly *Potamogeton natans,* range in common with water lilies. This species is not suitable for the aquarium but is well suited for garden pools and artificial lakes with spatterdocks.

● CULTIVATION: Plant species of water lilies in flowerpots or saucers with clayey earth, peat and leaf-mold. Add a quantity of charcoal and both inorganic and organic mud, which has been well dried in the sun. They need a good amount of light, especially direct sunshine, water of an acid or neutral reaction (pH 6.5-7.0) and temperatures from 68 to 82° F. in the summer are sufficient. Water lilies demand a rest period in winter. Dried rootstocks with their roots hibernate well in the cold with temperatures from 50 to 58° F. without water except for an occasional spraying at intervals of about 15 days. Plants which did

Hydrocotyle leucocephala, another Water Pennywort species for the home aquarium.

Hydrocotlye verticillata, note characteristic lobules of the leaves.

not get this hibernation flower very poorly. Propagate aquarium water lilies in a vegetative manner from leaf-buds, sometimes even by dividing the rootstock with a slice by a knife which is then covered with charcoal. The planting of seeds is another rather successful way used with most species. Take the usual steps, planting the seeds in damp sand and after the young plants come up, raise the water level.

Nymphoides aquatica (Banana Plant)

● DESCRIPTION: Perennial plant with a short stem. A bunch of green root tubercles grow from the short rootstock, looking like bananas or dahlia tubercles. These are organs where the plants gather their reserve substances. Leaves have petioles which are bright green or reddish with heart-shaped bases. Floating leaves are developed with red papillous petioles and stout blades which are dark green on the upper side and purple on the undersides and about 10 cm long.

A small white flower (1-2 cm in diameter) grows in the hollow of the leaves.

● ECOLOGICAL DATA: Banana plants grow in mild currents or shallow stagnant waters where rivers have overflowed, in warm or sunny places. It flourishes in the shallow water of an aquarium with floating plants like *Azolla* and *Salvinia,* as well as water milfoils and arrowheads.

● CULTIVATION: It makes no great demands as to the contents of the bottom: unwashed river sand with some mud is sufficient. The water should be clean but rich in nutritive substances. A temperature of 68 to 77° F. is sufficient and the light should fall directly from above.

Propagates by seeds which fall off on the water surface after ripening, but more frequently by the vegetative manner. Young plants spring from separated leaves or their cuttings.

Hydrocotyle vulgaris (Water Pennywort)

● DESCRIPTION: Grows mainly as a terrestrial form. It is a small perennial plant with thin trailing rooting stem, 10-40 cm long. Leaves are alternate, 10 cm long with a petiole that joins the leaf blade in the center. Its diameter is 1.5-4 cm and it is mildly dentate, hairless on the upper side and hairy on the underside. Flowers are small on short stalks, whitish or pink. The fruit is elliptic with the red diachenium divided in two parts.

Two aquatic forms are often found in the aquarium: *H. vulgaris forma natans* with floating leaves and *forma submersa.*

● ECOLOGICAL DATA: In its natural surroundings, it grows in peaty waters. In the aquarium, it is best to keep it toward the front under a slope of sand where detritus is more apt to gather together with plants like *Marsilia quadrifolia, Microsorium, Elodea densa, E. vivipara* and *Elatine macropoda.*

● CULTIVATION: Unwashed sand containing a bit of peat or clayey mud in tanks with mildly acid or neutral water and a sufficiency of light, these are the proper conditions for good growth of these plants which appear rather often in present-day aquaria. It does better in shallow tanks (maximum depth 15-25 cm).

Propagates by cuttings from the rootstock but also by planting seeds in damp sand with peat on saucers in shallow water.

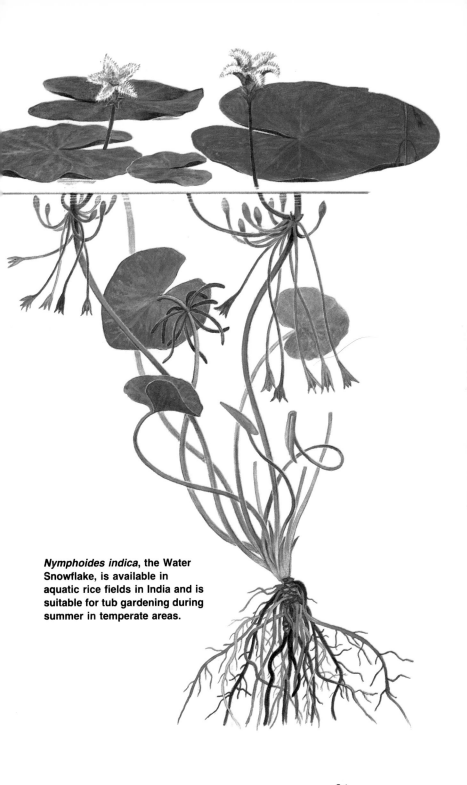

Nymphoides indica, the Water Snowflake, is available in aquatic rice fields in India and is suitable for tub gardening during summer in temperate areas.

Type 8 Plants

Bacopa amplexicaulis
- DESCRIPTION: Water or swamp plant with erect round stiff stem (60 cm long) which is only rarely branched. Leaves are opposed, with hairs on the underside (2-3 cm long, 1-1.5 cm wide), amplexicaul and elliptic. The stem is finely haired. Emersed leaves are stiffer, pulpy and bright. Stem and leaves give off an odor after they are rubbed.

  Flowering is above water, and the tubular or ball-shaped blooms grow from hollows of leaves on stems and are bright blue.
- ECOLOGICAL DATA: *Bacopa* tolerates species like *Sagittaria subulata*, *S. platyphylla*, *Ludwigia*, *Myriophyllum*, *Heteranthera*, *Micranthemum*, *Elodea* and *Lobelia*.
- CULTIVATION: The usual bottom is unwashed sand with detritus, perhaps a more nutritious clay, sand or earth mixture. The water should not be above 10 DH, and the temperature can fluctuate between 65 and 68° F. This plant requires a good deal of light. Plant bunches with several stems together. It propagates well by cuttings. Sometimes it dwarfs and perishes in warmer waters. If cultivated in the open in summer, it can be gotten to bloom more frequently.

Cabomba aquatica
- DESCRIPTION: A submersed aquatic plant with a richly branched stem which frequently attains a length of 2 m below the surface of the water. Leaves are opposed with petioles 2-4 cm long. The leaf blade is divided into fine green segments. It is 4-5 cm long and 4-7 cm wide, divided into 5 parts at the base and every part is divided 4 and 5 times again, giving each matured submersed leaf 80-150 segments. Submersed leaves form a rosette below the surface. Floating leaves are round, an appearance they get especially when flowering.

  The flower is bright yellow inside of the petals and green outside, arranged in threes (6 stamens, 3 ovaries).
- ECOLOGICAL DATA: This beautiful and decorative plant thrives best when grown alone. It tolerates some species of arrowheads which do not produce floating leaves on the surface and low species of *Echinodorus*.
- CULTIVATION: *Cabomba aquatica* is a rather sensitive aquarium plant. Add a clay mixture with peat to unwashed sand about 1:10, drying the clay in the sun first to prevent an excessive fermentative process. The water in the tank should be soft, under 6 DH, mildly acid with a pH value of 6.5-7.0. Keep the temperature from 73 to 77° F., not permitting a drop below 64° F. even in winter. There must always be a sufficiency of light with strong bulbs or fluorescent plant lights. Direct sunlight sometimes encourages a growth of algae on the plants. There is still one more circumstance which is important: This plant does not tolerate water motion, and for this reason plant it without any aeration or filtration. Propagate it by cutting off the growing tops and planting them about 5 cm deep in the bottom.

Limnophila heterophylla
- DESCRIPTION: An aquatic, submersed plant, generally used as an aquarium species. Thickly leaved stems to 50 cm long that produce green tufts. There are often long white roots in the nodes of the stems. The leaves are in whorls which usually average 6 to 8 and divide twice in

Cabomba piauhyensis, South
American species.

Cabomba caroliniana, North
American species.

Limnophila aquatica, grows in or out of water well.

the segments. The whorls are so thick at the ends that they form a rosette. The emersed parts of the stems have smaller leaves which are often stiff and sappy, dark green and sharply dentate, undivided (heterophylly).

Flowers are small, singly sessile in the axis of the leaves. They have 5 sepals, 5 white bilabiate petals, and are purple striped in the mouth.

● ECOLOGICAL DATA: A very decorative plant which does not make great demands. In the aquarium it makes a nice and typical association with the *Cryptocoryne* species, also with *Lagenandra, Rotala, Acorus, Vallisneria asiatica* and *V. gigantea.* It contrasts nicely to the dark green or brown leaves of the *Cryptocoryne* species. It prefers the lightest parts of the aquarium and frequently grows as high as the surface, especially with artificial lighting.

● CULTIVATION: All *Limnophila* species do not make great demands to growing conditions. Nevertheless it likes a sufficiency of light. The more light that falls on the plants the more decorative and healthy they are. It grows very well in the light of a 40 to 60 watt incandescent bulb. They seem to suffer only from bits of mud and detritus settling on the leaves. This causes the inferior parts of the stems to turn brownish, and the leaves sometimes fall off.

Add bits of dried clay to the rough sand in the aquarium bottom, but the detritus accumulation is usually sufficient nourishment. With a rather nutritious bottom, cultures often suffer from an abundance of epiphytical algae. That is why you should thin the thick tufts from time to time and plant the vegetative top in the new cultures.

Water temperatures should be in the higher ranges: 68 to 76° F. seem to be the preferred ranges. Water should be neutral to mildly acid (pH 6.5-7.0). Hardness is not decisive (5 to 25 DH) but it seems to prosper better in a mild water. As mentioned above, *Limnophila* propagates vegetatively from cuttings of the stems as well as by seeds.

Cardamine lyrata

- DESCRIPTION: Stems grow from a rootstock and are 15-30 cm high with opposed rounded egg-shaped or alternate leaves which are very fine. The leaf blade is bright green, translucent, and the petioles are thin. It produces intermediate forms with emersed leaves in shallow waters.

Terrestrial forms produce tall racemes of white flowers.

- ECOLOGICAL DATA: It shows a conspicuous contrast to the dark green color of *Vallisneria* and the milfoils in a cold-water aquarium. It can also be associated with *Sagittaria natans, Cailitriche, Elodea canadensis* and *Eleocharis acicularis.*
- CULTIVATION: Unwashed sand and water from 58 to 68° F. (rain water is best) are all that is needed for a good growth. Long white roots grow behind every leaf and you can propagate these plants easily by short cuttings under the leaves. It is a very fine and decorative plant which must be carefully protected from being overgrown by algae. Plant young vegetative tops by themselves. It is also possible to grow from seeds, which germinate readily in damp sand.

Rotala indica

- DESCRIPTION: *Rotala indica* is a submersed water plant 14-37 cm high. Leaves grow on short internodes and are oval, egg-shaped and opposed. Sometimes,

Rotala macrandra, light red to red colored leaves enhance appearance of this plant. Cultivation similar to R. indica.

especially with bright lighting, they are longitudinal, spoon-shaped and green to brownish red.

The flowers occur in the axis of emersed leaves and have a bell-shaped calyx with 4 sepals, 4 very small purplish violet petals and 4 stamens.

• ECOLOGICAL DATA: This plant does well with the Indo-Malayan *Cryptocoryne balansae, C. nevillii* and the fern *Microsorium pteropus.*

• CULTIVATION: It needs rougher sand with a sufficient quantity of organic mud (detritus). Lighting should be strong, preferably daylight. Water should be mildly acid to neutral (pH 6.5-7.0). Prefers a hardness from 4-15 DH measured in a tank with *Cryptocoryne* species. It is a very beautiful plant. Propagates easily by breaking off vegetative tops which are planted in bunches (always 3-4 plants) to form tufts. Located in the more dimly lighted places in the aquarium it forms bright green stems and smaller leaves.

Rorippa amphibia (Water Cress)

• DESCRIPTION: Swamp or semi-submersed plant, often producing submersed forms. The stem often trails below, 40-100 cm long and hollow. Leaves are longitudinal to lanceolate undivided but roughly dentate or with lobes, pinnatifid to pinnately lobed. The middle leaves are also undivided, dentate and narrowed down. The upper leaves are narrowed, longitudinal and sessile. Flowers are golden yellow.

• ECOLOGICAL DATA: This species is ecologically contingent on periodic fluctuation of the levels of pools and standing waters. In nature it comes in characteristic association with *Oeanthe aquatica* in swampy meadows with sedges and reeds. The submersed form tolerates *Veronica* and *Potamogeton* in the aquarium.

• CULTIVATION: This plant is more suitable for outdoor pools. It propagates quickly; accidental plants grow on leaves when they lodge on the bottom, especially in the summer dry period when the water level sinks.

An interesting plant which is suitable for biological studies both in nature and in tanks with other water plants.

Elatine macropoda

• DESCRIPTION: A small swamp or water plant with a trailing stem, often branched and rooting in the nodes. The leaves are small and spatulate, widening toward the point and narrowing toward the petiole. The leaf is 4.5-18 mm long and 2-3 mm wide, fine and bright green. The submersed varieties are green even in the winter.

This plant is known especially from aquarium culture, where it has been cultivated for a long time as a carpet-type plant that covers the bottom with a thick growth.

The flowers of the terrestrial forms are on stalks, with 4 sepals and 4 petals, 8 stamens and a ball-shaped ovary, and 4 stigmata. The fruit is ball-shaped.

• ECOLOGICAL DATA: *Elatine macropoda forma submersa* produces isolated growths on the sandy aquarium bottom and is a beautiful plant in a little tank by itself. It is also suited to be combined with the *Cryptocoryne* species, *Vallisneria, Hygrophila* and *Limnophila*. In the open it is known from the rice fields, where it is a good indicator of phosphorus and potassium. It does well also in a clay bottom.

Elodea canadensis (Anacharis)

CULTIVATION: A layer of sand with a good amount of detritus on the top proved to be a sufficiently good bottom for this plant. The water is better soft, preferably rain water, pH 6-6.5. It is not critical as to temperature and hibernates at temperatures as low as 64° F. *Elatine* also grows in aquaria with a high water level, 5-50 cm.

Iodea canadensis (Anacharis)
DESCRIPTION: A submerged water plant, 5-15 cm long, with a thickly leaved branched stem. The leaves are in whorls, rarely 2 to elongated, egg-shaped to near, lanceolate (2-3 mm wide and 5-10 mm long), translucent, dark green, finely serrated and pointed.

rassula helmsii, few rassulaceae live in water.

Flowers are bisexual in the hollows of leaves; they grow from the spathe and have long stalks; 3 sepals are concreted in a tube and broaden funnel-like reddish or green; 3 petals are round and whitish; 3 parts of the ovary remain in the spathe; 3 stigmae protrude from the flower, and the flower floats on the surface.

● ECOLOGICAL DATA: It was brought to Europe as a botanical rarity at the end of the 19th century. Today it is a very common plant which often produces impenetrable masses on the bottom of pools, ponds and other standing waters. Sometimes its numbers fluctuate periodically. A fast-growing plant without any great demands. In the cold-water aquarium, it grows in common with *Vallisneria spiralis*, *Ceratophyllum demersum* and *Potamogeton crispus*. It prefers eutrophic, alkaline water with a

Elatine
▼ macropoda

high percentage of calcium. It is also a suitable plant for outside pools with water lilies and spatterdocks.
● CULTIVATION: Plant it in the bottom of an aquarium in unwashed sand with a clay mud, not heated. It dies and turns brown with the higher temperatures. The water should be alkaline (pH 7.5-10), with a great deal of calcium. To provide this we add pieces of chalk, calcium carbonate or lime water into the tank. It demands direct light and propagates freely from segments of the stem.

Egeria densa

● DESCRIPTION: A stouter species than *E. canadensis*. The stem is sparsely branched, 3-4 m long with whorls with 3 or 4 leaves which are green and narrowly lanceolate. The blade is finely serrated on the side, 1.5-3 cm long and 3 mm wide.

There is one male flower growing from the spathe (2 cm long) and it protrudes on the stalk above the water; 3 sepals are small, greenish; 3 petals are small and colorless and there are 9 stamens. The petals of the female flower are 1-2 cm long.
● ECOLOGICAL DATA: This well known aquarium plant may be kept in a tank with other alkali-loving plants like *Myriophyllum pinnatum*, *M. hippuroides*, *M. heterophyllum*, *M.*

Egeria densa

proserpinacoides, Sagittaria subulata, Potamogeton gayi, Hydrilla verticillata and *Cabomba aquatica.*

Plant it only by itself for some tanks, especially breeding tanks.

- CULTIVATION: A bottom of unwashed sand is usually suitable, with a mixture of balls of calciferous clay mixtures and detritus. The water in the aquarium should be very alkaline, pH from 7 to 10 and hardness to 20-25 DH. Light intensity should always be adequate.

It adapts readily to the aquarium and withstands temperatures from 50 to 77° F., which is the usual range found in an unheated home aquarium. It propagates freely with good light conditions and shows great vitality in every plant; it also does well as a floating plant.

Zosterella dubia

- DESCRIPTION: A submersed perennial water plant. Its stem can attain 2 m, trailing or rooting in nodes. Leaves are opposed, bright green, 7-12 cm long and 0.5 cm wide, linear or ribbon-shaped, often broadened with an aerenchyma, especially the floating leaves (which makes the plant float in the water).

The yellow flowers are in the top of the axis on stalks 10 cm above the water, and the perianth consists of 6 petals, 3 stamens, with a perianth tube 1 to 7 cm long. Often called *Heteranthera dubia.*

ECOLOGICAL DATA: Found in common with *Heteranthera zosteraefolia, Ludwigia, Lobelia* and *Potamogeton gayi* in calciferous waters.

CULTIVATION: It prospers in alkaline water and is a strong, hardy plant. It tolerates temperatures down to 50° F., but plant it in tanks at temperatures

Elodea canadensis (Anacharis), see p.97.

from 65 to 75° F., as well as in the open. It propagates freely in the vegetative manner from cut stems and by seeds.

Heteranthera zosteraefolia

- DESCRIPTION: A perennial and submerged water plant. The stem

99

is up to 1 m high, trailing and branched. Numerous roots and leaves grow in nodes which are ribbon-shaped or ligulate, egg-shaped, oval, pointed, 3-5 cm long and 3-7 wide with three visible veins. The leaves are brigh green. Those that grow to the surface are rarely spoon-shaped and float on the water. Their blade is 2-4 cm long and 0.5 cm wide.

The bright blue flowers grow o stalks 1-2 cm long, above the water and frequently in pairs. Perianth leaves are very narrow, 4-7 mm long and 1 mm wide.
- ECOLOGICAL DATA: *H. zosteraefolia* does well with warm-water species like *Sagittaria subulata, Echinodorus cordifolius, E. berteroi,* and other species of *Zosterella.* It is a very decorative flower, especially when grown by itself when it produces beautiful, fresh green tufts in light spots.
- CULTIVATION: Plant the short thick parts of the stems in bunches of 4 or 5, because the lower leaves are very likely to turn brown and fall off. There are usually two periods of maximal growth during the year, in spring and in autumn. Its growth is very fast, and propagation is achieve by breaking off the tops carefully and planting them. The leaves are very fragile and easily broken. It usually grows in a sandy bottom with some mud or clay and neutral to alkaline water (pH 7-8) and a temperature 65 to 86° F. Water hardness is not important it grows in water from 5-20 DH.

Hottonia palustris (Water Violet)
- DESCRIPTION: A plant that floats in the water, with a branched stem, 20-60 cm long. Leaves and long white roots grow on the knots. The plant is rather

Bacopa monnieri, another well known aquarium plant cultivated by aquarists all over the world.

similar to the *Myriophyllum* species. Leaves are alternate, pinnately pectinated into linear cuts. Stems are whorl-like, branched at the surface where they form rosettes.

Flowers grow in bunches above the water surface in early spring, white or pink, with bracts which lengthen with the fruit, which is capsular.

● ECOLOGICAL DATA: It is typical of the plants that grow in the paludal meadows of Europe. It thrives in a paludal cold-water aquarium or in an open pool with plant species like *Hydrocharis morsus-ranae, Stratiotes, Potamogeton perfoliatus, P. lucens* and *Sparganium*.

Most likely it forms isolated formations, even in the rushes.
● CULTIVATION: A paludal aquarium with a low water level and a bottom of sand and some mud, possibly with some clay or peat added, is suitable for this beautiful and very interesting plant. The water should be cold, never exceeding 65° F. even in summer, neutral, about 6-10 DH. It forms winter buds (turions) in the autumn.
● CULTIVATION: A paludal aquarium with a low water level and a bottom of sand and some mud, possibly with some clay or peat added, is suitable for this beautiful and very interesting plant. The water should be cold, never exceeding 65°F. even in summer, neutral, about 6-10 DH. It forms winter buds (turions) in the autumn.

An interesting object for experiments which forms different leaf shapes when conditions change, it also changes the leaf colors and develops terrestrial forms.

Lindernia rotundifolia, resembles *Bacopa* greatly and grows under similar living conditions.

Hippuris vulgaris (Mare's Tail)

- DESCRIPTION: Perennial plant suggestive of a horse's tail or a little needle-leaved tree by its appearance. It grows paludal as well as aquatic forms. The rootstock trails, rooting in the mud, the stems are simple, 40 cm long when erect and 1 m long when floating, thickly leaved on short stalks. The leaves are 6-14 in number, in whorls, linear, 1-2 cm long, growing wider and shorter with emergent stems.

Flowers are very small, without any perianth and with a single stamen or pistil. The fruit consists of a tiny nut. It hibernates in winter and sprouts anew from the rootstock in spring.

- ECOLOGICAL DATA: A swamp terrarium or still better a pool with water vegetation like *Hydrocharis morsus-ranae, Nymphaea, Myriophyllum spicatum* or *M. verticillatum,* or the different rushes.

In nature it appears in flooded regions in waters rich in calcium. Sometimes it grows in beds as deep as 1.5 m.

- CULTIVATION: Sometimes plant this interesting plant in the aquarium as well, where it produces submerged variations at temperatures from 58 to 77° F. Water hardness fluctuates from 10-20 DH, and much light is required, especially daylight. You do not usually succeed in pulling *Hippuris* through the winter, because it usually dies.

Hydrilla verticillata

- DESCRIPTION: A submerged plant, very similar to the genus *Elodea.* The stem is 15-30 cm long and numerously branched. The leaves are linear, lanceolate, in whorls of 2 to 8, 10-20 mm long and 2-5 mm wide. They are dentate at the tip, the midrib is usually reddish, and there are 2 leaves at the base.

Heteranthera zosteraefolia, see p.99.

Facing page:

Left: *Acorus gramineus v. gramineus,* see p.29.

Center: *Zosterella dubia,* typical aquatic plant from Mexico, Cuba and southern United States.

Right: *Acorus gramineus v. gramineus fol. variegatis.*

Hydrilla verticillata,
see p.102.

The flowers are bisexual, arranged in threes and the male flowers are in a ball-shaped spathe; after ripening they split up and float on the surface, where pollination occurs. The female flowers are small, without stalks, and the lower part of the perianth is elongated into a tube which touches the surface with its upper, broadened part. It is 2-3 cm long. The fruits are tubular with 5 seeds, green and slimy.

● ECOLOGICAL DATA: It does well in a cold-water aquarium when kept with *Elodea, Vallisneria spiralis, Hygrophila, Ottelia alismoides* and the *Potamogeton* species. The dark green color of *Hydrilla* forms a pleasing contrast to the others. It is also suitable for garden pools; it grows well in standing, shallow and cold water. Sometimes its growth is restrained by *Elodea canadensis.*

● CULTIVATION: This fine plant, which must above all be protected from an excessive growth of algae, does well in a cold-water aquarium. It makes no special demands as to the bottom, a usual mixture of unwashed sand with some earth being sufficient. The temperature may fluctuate from 64 to 75° F. Water hardness should be about 8-10 DH. *Hydrilla* produces turions (winter buds) for hibernation. Of course, the tropical species prefer higher temperatures and are more suitable for our aquaria. In any case the *Hydrilla* species are highly varied and very interesting. It propagates easily from stem cuttings. Escapes cultivation readily.

Lagarosiphon major

• DESCRIPTION: Very similar in appearance to the genus *Elodea*, but differs by its leaves, which are not in whorls but single in flat spirals and crispate. The stems are erect, thickly leaved and up to 1 m long, often very fragile. The leaves are 1.5-2 cm long, and 2 mm wide, dark green and mildly crispate on the sides of the blade, the leaf axils bearing 2 minute scales. A midrib is green. The male flowers grow from the spathe to the water surface and float freely on the turned-back petals. Three stamens make the anthers horizontal. Each of them contains 16 yellow pollen grains. The next 3 stamens protruding up are sterile. The female flowers grow to the water surface and are pollinated by the touch of the anthers of the male flowers. The pollen falls on the stigmae without getting any contact with the water. Pollination is similar to that of the genus *Hydrilla*.

Flowers only if the plants have artificial lighting 10-12 hours a day.

• ECOLOGICAL DATA: *Lagarosiphon* grows well with *Vallisneria spiralis, Aponogeton natans, Ceratopteris thalicroides, Chara, Nitella* and *Ludwigia*.

• CULTIVATION: The usual bottom with unwashed sand and an addition of organic mud or aquarium detritus. It demands a good amount of calcium and potassium in the water. Add calcareous clay and artificial fertilizers when the plant is in full growth. It requires a lot of light, especially in winter. The water should be neutral to mildly alkaline, pH value 7-8.5 and water hardness 10-15 DH. The plant makes no great demands as to water temperature, and fluctuations from 54 to 65° F. are possible.

Lagarosiphon muscoides = *Lagarosiphon major*

Hygrophila polysperma

• DESCRIPTION: The aquatic form has a stem that is up to 50 cm long, with few leaves. Leaves are opposed and have a very variable shape, bright green, elongated, egg-shaped, 4 cm long and 1.5 cm wide. The leaves of the emergent forms are narrower and dark green.

The flowers are sessile in the axils of emergent leaves and 2 bracts, covered with hairs, are 5-15 mm long. Sepals are pointed, consisting of 5 parts, and petals are white or bluish with two lips. The upper lip has two lobes and the lower one has three. There are two stamens. The fruit is a capsule 6-12 mm long with 20-30 seeds. The flowers appear rarely, and this plant is easier to propagate from cuttings, especially in the aquarium.

- ECOLOGICAL DATA: It is a notable representative of the Indo-Malayan region like the *Cryptocoryne* species, *Ceratopteris thalicoides, Acorus* and *Hygrophila corymbosa*. It forms bright green tufts which grow to the surface with good light. The plant is also suitable in shallow-water pools in the summertime.

- CULTIVATION: The plant has no particular demands as to bottom, being very hardy and adaptive. Sand with a little mud and clay added is sufficient for 2-3 years of good growth when left alone. It is important to say here that this plant makes a marked change in the concentration of hydrogen ions in the tank and after some time it has a tendency to turn neutral water into water with an acid reaction. Therefore it does not have a great tolerance for plants that have need for alkaline water. It has rather considerable claims as to light but grows well with artificial lighting. The optimum temperature is 64 to 77° F., but extreme temperatures of 54 and 86° F. have been endured without any visible damage. It grows well in soft water but can also adapt to hard conditions.

Every part of the plant or leaf if broken off roots at once in the water and grows into a new plant, making it no problem to propagate this plant in the aquarium.

Lobelia cardinalis (Water Lobelia)

- DESCRIPTION: A submersed water form. The stem is thick, round, erect, 10 to 30 cm long. Leaves are alternate, 2-6 cm long and 1-1.5 cm wide, short with an oval petiole. The blade is usually swollen, not flat and with a bright green midrib.

In soft water or mud it produces terrestrial forms which have a long (up to 1 m) flowering stalk with bright red flowers and a bell-shaped corolla.

- ECOLOGICAL DATA: A plant which can be kept with the species of *Ludwigia, Potamogeton gayi, Micranthemum nuttalii* and *Vallisneria americana*. Sometimes it even tolerates species of the genus *Sagittaria*.

- CULTIVATION: In summer it prospers in the open air in the mud but in the aquarium it is also suitable for heated tanks. A mixture of clay and unwashed sand proved to be good for this species. It is spread among aquarists, but with the shortage of light it produces long starved forms which lose their leaves. It demands a rest in winter, hibernating at the lower temperature of about 68° F. very well. It prefers toplight, a pH value 6.5-7.0 and water hardness 8-12 DH.

Ludwigia arcuata

- DESCRIPTION: A perennial paludal plant with a reddish colored stem. Its leaves are lanceolate and opposed, 1-2.5 cm long and about 0.5 cm wide, pointed at the tip and emerald green. The stems grow above the water and in the terrestrial form the leaves are much smaller, the stems are thickly overgrown with leaves and more intensely colored, often overhanging and flowering.

Hygrophila difformis,
see p.115.

Hygrophila polysperma, see
p.105.

107

The flowers are small, golden yellow, stalkless, sessile on emergent leaves on the stalks. The calyx is bell-shaped, with 4 corners, petals are dentate, there are 4 stamens and 1 ovary in the flower. The fruit is a capsule with 4 cases.

● ECOLOGICAL DATA: In the aquatic phase it does well in an unheated tank with *Potamogeton gayi*, *Lobelia cardinalis* and *Ludwigia palustris*. It produces branched forms with small leaves in a thickly overgrown tank. In its terrestrial form it prefers to grow by itself even in a flowerpot, where it often flowers.

● CULTIVATION: *Ludwigia arcuata* demands these conditions for its successful culture: a sandy bottom with a mixture of mud and garden earth (a leaf-mold or a sod-mold) which should be mixed with the sand in a proportion of 1 to 10. *Ludwigia* demands a great deal of light, especially in the emergent and flowering phase. Even in a glasshouse it does best in the lightest spot at the windows. In winter it is best to let the temperatures sink to 54 to 58° F. because the plant demands a period of rest. Temperatures of 59 to 77° F. are right for the summer. Hardness of the water seems to make little difference.

It propagates well by seeds and also vegetatively (by cutting the highest part of the stems). But of course, vegetative cutting and propagation can be recommended only in the summer months. In the winter months, the cuttings root very poorly.

All of the *Ludwigia* species have the habit of shedding their lower leaves at the beginning of the winter period, especially in a heated tank. Before they fall off, the brown necrotic spots appear on the leaves. This is surely

Rotala rotundifolia,
Indian species.

Ludwigia repens
▼

▲
**Ludwigia arcuata, see
p. 106.**

connected with the vegetative rhythm. In the spring propagate *Ludwigia* by cutting off the highest parts of the stems again or plant seeds in shallow sand.

Ludwigia palustris

● DESCRIPTION: A swamp or water plant with a thick articulated stem, divided, sometimes ledged, 15-30 cm long. Leaves are opposed, sessile or with short petioles pointed on the end. They are 2-5 cm long and 2 cm wide. The blade is smooth and thick, bright green on the upper side and dark olive to violet on the reverse.

The flower is formed by 4 sepals, united and bell shaped, yellowish green in color. There are no petals but 4 stamens. The fruit is hemisphere-shaped and has 4 longitudinal green wrinkles.

● ECOLOGICAL DATA: In the aquarium *L. palustris var. submersa* may be placed with *Sagittaria*, *Myriophyllum scabratum* and *M. heterophyllum*, *Vallisneria americana* and *Nuphar advena*.

● CULTIVATION: Same as with *L. arcuata* but this species does not require as much light and is more acclimated to aquarium life than the other *Ludwigia* species.

Lysimachia nummularia (Loosestrife)

● DESCRIPTION: A hygrophilous, often inundated plant which can produce submerged forms. Stems are 4-20 cm long, four-cornered, rooting in the nodes. Projections are up to 1 m in length. Leaves are opposed, widely egg-shaped, undivided with a short petiole and red dots.

Flowers are yellow, with dark red dots inside, with 5 sepals, 5 petals, and 5 stamens. The fruit is a capsule.

Myriophyllum (Water Milfoils)

● ECOLOGICAL DATA: This is a plant from a mild zone, where it appears in inundated meadows, ditches and brooks in common with *Veronica beccabunga, Rorippa, Callitriche* and *Myriophyllum* or in rushes on swampy earth in common with *Typha* and *Phragmites,* in some places even with *Glyceria fluitans.*

● CULTIVATION: This plant produces a submerged form, suitable for aquarium conditions where it even grows rather well in unwashed sand. It thrives better in soft water with a mixture of some mud, but it is also suitable for terrariums and garden pools. It does not demand a great deal of heat, neither does it insist on a lot of light. It acclimates quite readily even when we transplant specimens from the open into house aquaria.

Temperature 50 to 68° F., pH value 6.8-7.0, water hardness 6-20 DH are sufficient for this hardy plant, which should be used and studied more in the aquarium.

Myriophyllum (Water Milfoils)

Water milfoils are submerged aquatic plants distributed almost all over the world (about 40 species), mainly in cold water in the southern hemisphere, but common in the U.S.A. as well. Many species grow in Australia, but they form a special group which are not cultivated in the aquarium.

Milfoils have single, sometimes thinly branched stems. Leaves are alternate or opposed; in the case of aquatic species they are most often arranged in whorls and are divided into linear segments. The emerged leaves of bog forms are pinnate or serrate. Flowers are minute, mostly in the axes of leaf petioles or arranged in fine spikes. Fruits are achenes or small nuts, characteristic for each species. This is important for identification.

The habits of aquarium water milfoils conform to an underwater life. They are very decorative, of a delicate appearance, and create a green tangle with their fine linear leaf segments, very suitable for fishes and their fry because they are hosts to numerous plankton. Such plants are also an important source of "oxygen" in the tank. They do best in larger aquaria with peaceful fishes and a minimum of water disturbance. It is necessary to protect the leaves from a settling of fine particles; clean them occasionally by gently shaking them from time to time.

Like several other aquarium plants milfoils remain in sterile corms. Although they reach a comparatively fair size in a large tank, often up to 1-2 m, they never flower in it and thus are sterile. Neither in a greenhouse will you ever observe any flowers. They multiply almost exclusively in a vegetative way: by cuttings, segments and vegetative tops which root easily after being planted in the bottom sand. Fill the aquarium bottom with coarse unwashed river sand 5-10 cm high and plant cuttings or young plants with roots in groups of 5 or 6. This first layer should be covered with 2-3 cm of fine well-washed river sand. When washing this, it is well to use boiling water to reduce the growth of algae. Otherwise algae may spread very quickly in the newly set-up tank. Another natural way of clearing the water, and the most advisable one, is to introduce some live daphnia. Then, of course, the fish must be left out. Another good method to prevent contamination is to disinfect plants, decorations and stones with a very dilute (pale pink) potassium permanganate solution for 20 to 30 minutes.

The night motions of young vegetative tops in the evening are very interesting. Leaves on a top part of the stem close when the light gets dim; these motions are especially conspicuous with the species of M. brasiliense.

Milfoils like alkaline water with a pH value about 7.7-8.0 containing an abundant amount of dissolved organic and inorganic substances and a high content of calcium ions. Add organic fertilizers, hydroponic solutions and chalk (calcium). If there is more than enough calcium it is eliminated as a carbonate on the surface of plants (incrustation). Fertilize the water only in summer.

Water milfoils require a good amount of light. If shaded or in a thickly overgrown tank the lower leaf whorls fall off and poorly developed green "starved forms" result. These plants also demand a sufficient amount of room. Protect branching of stems by cutting off vegetative tops.

Otherwise they are very hardy and well suited for beginners; they grow well even in unheated tanks at temperatures of 59 to 68° F.

Myriophyllum spicatum

● DESCRIPTION: Myriophyllum spicatum is a plant that occurs in ponds, lakes and pools. It can grow as long as 2-3 m, rooting in the bottom. Leaves are arranged in whorls that consist of 4 (sometimes 5 or 6) pinnate leaves, and the segments are threadlike and may be 35 cm long. Bracts undivided in spike, shorter than flowers. Rich, thick spikes, elongated, produce flowers in whorls. The spike extends above the water and has 8 stamens. The fruit is an achene

Right: Myriophyllum mattogrossense, red leaved species. Left: Myriophyllum aquaticum = M. brasiliense (Parrot's feather), see p. 113.

Limnophila sessiliflora, needs intense lighting.

up to 3 mm in diameter. Flowers are anemophilous, the pollen being transferred by wind. Fruits ripen only rarely, so this plant usually multiplies in a vegetative manner by fragments. *M. spicatum* is olive green, stems are wine-red or brownish, sometimes colored more strongly in a light locality.

● ECOLOGICAL DATA: *M. spicatum* grows in tufts both in standing and flowing water in association with *Potamogeton* and sometimes *Ranunculus* and *Ceratophyllum demersum,* as well as *Nuphar luteum.* The association of *M. spicatum* with tropical species of the same genus in the aquarium has not yet been thoroughly studied.

● CULTIVATION: Use river sand with an addition of mud rich in decaying organisms and calcium. This usually results in some incrustation. The water should be hard with a high percentage of calcium from ponds or pools. Much light is required.

Myriophyllum verticillatum

● DESCRIPTION: An aquatic plant rarely producing terrestrial forms. Stem is bright to brownish green, 50-300 cm long, narrowed where whorls appear; internodes are 2-3 cm long, the inferior part of the stem with many hibernating buds and rootstock trailing in the mud with numerous roots. There are 4, sometimes 5 leaves in whorls which divide into threadlike segments. Cylindrical multicellular trichomes appear on young leaves. Length and shape of leaves depend on the amount of nutritive substances in the bottom and in the water, and the amount of current there. Segments are finer and longer in standing waters and in the aquarium.

Small flowers are sessile at the

base of bracts on spikes above the water surface. These occur in June and July. There are female flowers in the lower part of the inflorescence, bisexual in the middle and male flowers with white stamens on top. Fruits are ball-shaped, quadri-dentate splitting up into 4 parts. Promotive bracts on floral spikes are pectinately pinnated (unlike *M. spicatum*).

● ECOLOGICAL DATA: *M. verticillatum* grows in pools of the lowlands and warmer regions, in common with *Nuphar luteum, Ceratophyllum demersum, Potamogeton crispus, P. acutifolius, Hydrocharis morsus-ranae, Lemna trisulca* and *L. minor. M. verticillatum* avoids places where the calcium content is high and the milfoils are represented by *M. spicatum*.

● CULTIVATION: Bottom should consist of a fine river sand with some organic mud; the water should be clear, without chlorine, and alkaline, pH value 7.5-8.0, containing a generous amount of food substances, warmer than for the species *M. spicatum* and *M. alternifolium,* 59 to 72° F. In the open this species seems to be distributed in waters where the calcium is high, but it does not appear in acid waters at all. Hardness of the water should be 5-10 DH.

In the aquarium it often produces hibernating buds on the lower part of the stem. It propagates vegetatively from stem parts but does not seem to be as long-lived as *M. spicatum*.

Myriophyllum brasiliense (Parrot's Feather)

● DESCRIPTION: A stout paludal or submerged aquatic plant with a stem up to 1.5 m long, rarely branched. Leaves are in groups of 4-6 in whorls, 3-5 cm long, divided into 4-8 bright green segments (1 cm long); on the sides of the leaf there is a rachis. Stems with leaves above water are stiff, the leaves shorter, succulent bluish green, covered with tiny glands that give a velvety shine.

The flowers on short stalks are in the axis of emergent leaves, the female flowers below and the male flowers above with 4 white or rosy petals. Fruit is oval, consisting of 4 parts, with short stalks, pointed and covered with papillae.

● ECOLOGICAL DATA: This milfoil species is the one usually planted in aquaria. It can be kept in the aquarium with many species of *Echinodorus* and *Sagittaria.* It is well suited also for the terrarium because of its amphibious character (it often grows out of the water).

● CULTIVATION: The usual bottom for the other milfoils is suitable for cultivation. It grows better at higher temperatures (66 to 77° F.) in neutral to strongly alkaline water (pH 7-10) and with a hardness up to 16 DH. The water should be at least 40 cm deep, otherwise it is likely to develop the emerged form which is unsuitable for the aquarium because of its low leaf whorls which would brown and fall off.

Micranthemum umbrosum, **prefers emerse condition.**

When the bottom is low in nourishment, it sends out large roots and produces large whorls if the water is deep. In heated tanks, it produces quite another form with smaller leaves and less frequent whorls.

Potamogeton gayi

● DESCRIPTION: A perennial water plant with thin long and trailing rootstocks, richly branched. The roots are long and thread-like. The stem is brownish green, richly branched (especially on top), 50-100 cm long. Leaves are linear, narrowed on the base, bluntly pointed and alternate. They are 3-7 cm long, 3-4 mm wide and stipulate.

The leaves and stems are brownish red in a bright location, and form thick growths below the surface.

The inflorescence is a spike with several flowers, 6 cm long.

● ECOLOGICAL DATA: Can be grown together with *Ludwigia, Heteranthera, Lobelia cardinalis* and *Riccia fluitans,* floating on the water surface in the aquarium.

● CULTIVATION: Plant *Potamogeton gayi* in the aquarium with a shallow layer of unwashed sand (mixed with about 1 part in 10 of clay or mud). This plant requires a great deal of light and grows well even with artificial light. Temperatures should be from 65 to 77° F., water neutral to slightly alkaline, pH 7-8.5 and the hardness 9 to 15 DH.

An undemanding aquarium plant, suitable for beginners. It grows especially well by itself with a free water surface and becomes richly branched below. It propagates easily in a vegetative manner by runners and stem segments. When the light does not suit it, the lower leaves drop off and the tops lose color. These same signs become evident when the water is too cold.

Hygrophila corymbosa

Hygrophila difformis

● DESCRIPTION: Amphibious perennial plant with long roots that even grow on the lower part of the stem. Submersed stems are 40-80 cm long and sporadically hairy and frequently branched; they are always erect at the end and aromatic. Internodes are 2-7 cm long and shortened at the top so that the upper leaves form a rosette. Opposed leaves are bright green, whitish on the underside with short petioles, their shapes are very variable. At first they are oval, egg-shaped to lanceolate, undivided; later they become dentate and cut out, even when only 5 cm long. More mature leaves are up to 12 cm long, pinnately to deeply lobed. You often find all of the leaf types on a single stem.

The inflorescence, sessile on the axes in the hollows of bracts, consists of 1-3 flowers. One of the 5 sepals is usually longer (5 mm), the bright violet corolla is tubular, 10-12 mm long with the upper lip consisting of two parts and the lower of three parts. The interior is dark violet and corrugated. There are four stamens and one ovary. The fruit consists of a single capsule with many seeds. Formerly called *Synnema triflorum.*

● ECOLOGICAL DATA: Will tolerate other plants from the same region, such as *Cryptocoryne, Limnophila* and *Ceratopteris.* Besides these, *Hygrophila polysperma* can also be grown here.

● CULTIVATION: This plant propagates excellently in a vegetative manner from all parts of the stem. Also, leaves floating on the surface put out roots in a short time. Easily propagates by cuttings, dividing the rootstock, as well as runners and leaves.

Hygrophila guianensis

Nitella flexilis (Stonewort)

- DESCRIPTION: A green stonewort alga, with a thallus that is divided in rhizoids, consisting of many cells, stems and leaves which are arranged in periodic whorls. Cellular membrane consists of two layers, the outer one usually encrusted with calcium carbonate.

Organs of reproduction arise in nodes, both male and female organs on the same plant. Genetically stoneworts are very old plant types, traces of the genera *Chara* and *Nitella* having been found as far back as the Devonian.

- ECOLOGICAL DATA: Found in eutrophic waters, shallow and sandy pools as well as brackish waters with a calcium content in common with *Chara*, *Ceratophyllum* and *Myriophyllum spicatum*, it sometimes produces large growths similar to water meadows. It is a useful plant in fish-breeding hatchery pools.

- CULTIVATION: It is also a very valuable plant in the aquarium. Grow it by itself and remove as much as is needed whenever the occasion arises. Vegetative propagation is done by tubercles, isolated buds and stem branching. It is also possible to propagate by spores. The water should have a great concentration of calcareous compounds and an alkaline reaction (pH 7.5-9.0) with the water hardness 15-25 DH. All stoneworts are indicators of chemical water pollution and perish in a short time if any exists. A temperature of 42 to 86° F. is tolerated. If grown in a strong light, stoneworts are often attacked by algae.

Fontinalis antipyretica

- DESCRIPTION: A water moss with stems 20-50 cm long, branched, with leaves. These leaves are dark olive green to brownish, deeply keeled. They are 8 mm long and 4 mm wide. The whole stem is thickly leaved in 3 rows.

A sporogonium with a capsule grows only rarely with the aquatic form. The little rhizoids cling to the bottom by their false rootlets. *Fontinalis antipyretica* develops many forms and varieties; it is a very variable species.

- ECOLOGICAL DATA: It is usually found in cold flowing water, stalkless on the stones. Often in common with green algae and other mosses in brooks, ditches and lakes.

- CULTIVATION: Does not usually do well in a heated aquarium; it loses the green color of its leaves, which turn brown and die. Tufts are usually transferred from their native waters to the aquarium, because it is a very suitable plant for breeding tanks. It is advisable to rinse it well first under the tap to cut down on undesirable parasites. It is best to transfer this moss if possible on the stone where it grew. The best place to collect plants is in the warmer lowland waters. If you succeed in keeping it in the aquarium for a longer time, you will find that the leaves often change their shape. They are smaller and the stems are more elongated. The plant is suitable for breeding tanks: many fish species like to deposit their eggs in it.

Propagating this plant is possible only by dividing the old clumps.

Vesicularia dubyana (Java Moss)

- DESCRIPTION: A tropical water moss of a very variable shape. Stems are irregularly branched, creating thick tufts with two rows of leaves. These are lanceolate,

**Vesicularia dubyana
(Java Moss).**

Ceratopteris thalicroides (Water Sprite)

small, 10-14 mm long and 5-7 mm wide. Water forms often develop a sporogonium with capsule. Emersed they form tufts on stones, stumps or a damp soil; the tufts are fixed by rhizoids. Leaves are bright, widely lanceolate and deep green.

• ECOLOGICAL DATA: Java moss will associate with other Malayan plants such as the *Cryptocoryne* species, as well as *Limnophila, Acorus, Vallisneria asiatica* and *Ceratopteris*.

• CULTIVATION: Sessile on stones, wood, peat, or even glass as an epiphyte. It seems to propagate more readily in damp glasshouses where the water level is raised gradually. Sometimes it propagates poorly or even dies when left under water. Otherwise it is an ideal aquarium plant for small aquaria, especially when fish are being bred. It tolerates any water and grows even in the worst light conditions and is easy to clean by rinsing in running water. It can even be squeezed out gently to get rid of the sludge that gathers on the small leaves.

Mix peaty water for cultivation; it should be acid (pH 5.5) to neutral (pH 7.0) with a low hardness (3-4 DH). Rain water is the most suitable. Unwashed sand is mixed with peat moss (1:10) and the water temperature should range from 62 to 78° F. Watch closely for growths of epiphytic algae; it is very difficult to get rid of them, and often even a long-term cultivation in acid conditions is of no help.

Ceratopteris thalicroides (Water Sprite)

• DESCRIPTION: An annual water fern, 50-70 cm high, its axis and leaves reduced in a rosette. It produces a floating form and emersed leaves of varied shapes.

Roots are thick and in bunches. Leaves have short or long petioles; sometimes the blade is undivided but it can also be lobed. Leaf segments are round at the point. Leaves are fragile and break off easily, 45 cm long and 25 cm wide. Emersed leaves (sporophyls) are divided in filiform segments and they bear ball-shaped sporangia on the underside in 1-2 rows lengthwise. Occasional buds arise on the leaves, especially when submersed or floating, and new plants develop from them. Leaves are dark green to emerald green. Emersed sporophyls are brownish green in bright light.

• ECOLOGICAL DATA: A cosmopolitan tropical fern which is suitable to be kept with the genera *Cryptocoryne, Acorus, Limnophila, Cabomba, Ludwigia, Heteranthera* and *Vallisneria*.

• CULTIVATION: *Ceratopteris thalicroides* is a frequently cultivated, popular and very quick-growing aquarium fern. Nevertheless it is not always easy to get beautiful erect specimens under the artificial conditions found in the aquarium. This plant has certain specific requirements as to light, bottom and temperature.

Always add peat in mixture with unfertilized garden earth to unwashed rough sand (1:10). Bright light is best, but artificial light also gets good results. Temperatures should not drop below 68° F. even in the winter. Best temperatures are between 68 and 78° F. This plant prefers rather highly acid conditions: pH value should be 5-6.5 and soft water, always under 10 DH, preferably 5-6 DH. Propagates well in a vegetative manner by buds on leaves.

Plant it so that the leaf buds are above the sand.

◄ *Ceratopteris cornuta*

Ceratopteris thalicroides ►

Leptodictyum riparium, water moss similar to *Fontinalis antipyretica* (see p.116) but more durable and tolerates warmer water.

Microsorium pteropus

● DESCRIPTION: Aquatic or terrestrial, often periodically inundated fern which grows along the shore. It has a strong, green, scaly rootstock with numerous fine hairs (trichomes) and long roots.

Leaves have short petioles 5-6 cm wide and 10-30 cm long, lanceolate, undivided, bright green often with brown spots of necrotic tissue. It propagates in a vegetative manner by producing leaf buds on the sides of the leaves.

Emersed leaves (sporophyls) have three lobes with rows of spores along the underside of the midrib. The leaf blade is corrugated, characteristically concave in some places with a conspicuous nervation.

● ECOLOGICAL DATA: In the aquarium it can be kept with the *Cryptocoryne* species as well as *Acorus, Ceratopteris* and *Limnophila.*

● CULTIVATION: Never plant *Microsorium* in sand; merely fix it to stumps or roots with a fine thread. It will soon cling to these by its roots and form thick tufts.

There should be a sufficiency of peat in the bottom; the water should be neutral to acid (pH 5.5-7.0) and the hardness 6-8 DH. It makes no great demands as to light, and a medium intensity is sufficient as well as an artificial source, fluorescent tubes or incandescent bulbs.
Temperatures between 68 and 83° F. are tolerated. It takes some time, often 1-2 months, before beginning to propagate and grow new leaves. It grows very well in a small glasshouse, in an empty aquarium or on damp peat. It is a beautiful and very decorative plant and is fairly well known among aquarium and terrarium hobbyists.

Marsilea quadrifolia (Four-leaved Water Clover)

**Marsilea quadrifolia (Four-
leaved Water Clover)**
● DESCRIPTION: A small water
fern which produces two types of
spores. The rootstock is 50-100
cm long and trails in the mud with
two rows of leaves on the back
with long petioles (to 80 cm) with
a quaternate blade similar to the
clover or wood-sorrel. The young
leaves are usually downy, later
bare, widely wedge-shaped,
rounded on the sides. The
sporocarps are ball-shaped, felt-
like, and the spores are used in
determining the individual
Marsilea species.
● ECOLOGICAL DATA: In nature
Marsilea is found in association
with *Eleocharis acicularis* in an
inundated zone at the water's
edge, where it also develops the
terrestrial form when the water
recedes. In the aquarium it does
well in company with
Cryptocoryne and *Vallisneria*
species, but prefers to grow in a
half-submerged form in a shallow
aquarium in common with other
amphibious ferns or mosses and
also *Acorus gramineus.*
● CULTIVATION: All the species
of the genus *Marsilea,* known as
the "quatrefoils," are good
aquarium plants. They prefer a
fine sand or a clay-sand mixture
which makes the water more acid.
A peat bottom is also good with
the temperatures 58 to 72° F., pH
value 6.5-7 and the water
hardness 6-10 DH. These plants
do not require a great deal of light
and also grow in the shady parts
of the aquarium.
　　The plant may be propagated
by dividing the rootstock and
weighing down the ends. The
young leaves are spirals on the
stem ends.

**Marsilea hirsuta, Australian in ▶
origin.**

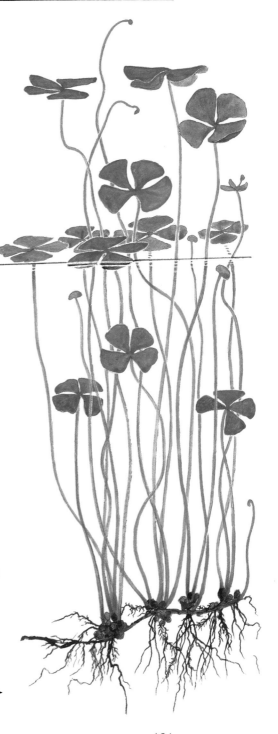

Ceratophyllum demersum (Hornwort)

▲ *Ceratophyllum demersum* (Hornwort), see p.25.

▲ *Alternanthera reineckii*, attractive marsh plant that prefers submersed situation.

◄ *Saururus cernuus,* two growth forms shown here, see p.125.

Cardamine lyrata, see p.95.
▼

Bolbitis heteroclita,
Asian water fern
cultivated like
**Microsorium
pteropus**

Type 10 Plants

Saururus cernuus
- DESCRIPTION: A bog plant, often growing to 1 m in length with a richly branched rootstock that trails in the mud. Stems are erect, round, hairy in their lower parts and bare above. Opposed leaves have petioles 8-12 cm long, hairy at first and then becoming bare as the leaves get older. Blades are heart-shaped, 10-15 cm long and 6-8 cm wide with an elongated point. The upper side of the leaf is dark green and dotted. Venation consists of 7 primary veins.

The flowers appear in a spiked inflorescence, whitish-yellow, stipulate, having 6 stamens and 3-4 stigmas. Fruits are ball-shaped.
- ECOLOGICAL DATA: In the open in the summertime, they are found with shore swamp plants like *Sparganium, Eleocharis, Acorus* and *Cyperus.*
- CULTIVATION: Propagates very quickly by runners and tends to crowd out other plants. It also does well in a sandy bottom, and the species from the northern zones can even hibernate in the open. It is also cultivated as a house plant for decoration of stands with aquaria, like *Cyperus.* At one time it was in frequent use as an aquarium plant, but nowadays it is cultivated only in terrraria and natural pools.

Limnocharis flava
- DESCRIPTION: A perennial swamp plant. The lanceolate or egg-shaped leaves with a long petiole and sheath grow from the short rootstock. The blade is 15 cm long and 12 cm wide. The base of the leaf is heart-shaped at times.

The inflorescence consists of an umbel of 2-12 yellow flowers with a membranous sheath, 1.5 cm in diameter.
- CULTIVATION: Paludal aquaria or terraria, in summer garden pools, in association with plants like *Pontederia cordata, Orontium aquaticum* and *Eichhornia crassipes.*
- CULTIVATION: In shallow water on a swampy bottom it can be kept the year round at temperatures 68 to 77° F. It flowers in summer during July and August, the shoots, which root easily, often appearing in the hollows of floral bracts. Can also be propagated by dividing the rootstock.

It prefers direct sunshine, water of neutral or mildly acid reaction (pH 6.8-7.0), and a water hardness 5-15 DH.

Sparganium ramosum (Bur Reed)
- DESCRIPTION: Swamp and water plant that has a strong rootstock with projections. Stem is erect, fruit bent behind, leaves are stiff, three-edged below and keel-shaped at the point, 3-15 mm wide. Flower stem is branched.
- CULTIVATION: This species is suitable for artificial lakes and pools as a bog plant in zones of rushes. *Sparganium ramosum* thrives in muddy earth 30-60 cm deep. Propagates quickly by long runners, especially when the depth varies.

It grows in ditches, near river banks and alongside ponds and lakes. It is not suitable for fish ponds, where it is a pest because its thick growth takes much nutriment and aids in overgrowing the water.

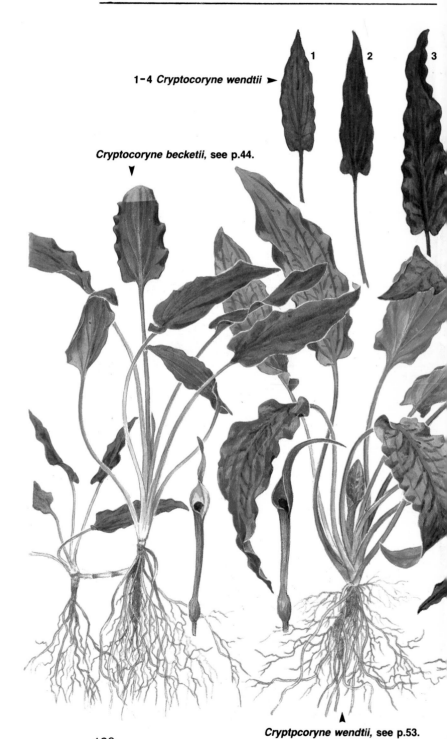

1–4 *Cryptocoryne wendtii* ➤

Cryptocoryne becketii, see p.44.

Cryptpcoryne wendtii, see p.53.

4

Cryptocoryne walkeri = lutea ▼

Cryptocoryne undulata ▲

Flower of *Crinum thaianum*, another popular Crinum.

Crinum natans, aquatic representative of the Amaryllis family.